# The Long Walk Home

An expanded edition of

# The Long Walk Home
*An escape in wartime Italy*

## PETER MEDD & FRANK SIMMS

with additional material from Andrew Adams,
Marcus Binney and Frank Simms

SICKLE MOON BOOKS

First published in Great Britain by John Lehmann in 1951

This edition published by Sickle Moon Books
61 Exmouth Market, London EC1R 4QL in 2019

Copyright Preface & Appendix © Andrew Adams, 2019
Copyright Afterword © Marcus Binney, 2019

ISBN 978 1 900209 23 6

A full CIP record for this book is available from the
British Library

Cover images: *The Village of Sillico in the Garfagnana, Tuscany*,
by permission of the Comune di Pieve Fosciana, Garfagnana,
with portraits of Frank Simms and Peter Medd superimposed

Text set in Great Britain by James Morris
Printed by Clays Ltd, Elcograf S.p.A

# CONTENTS

# PREFACE TO THE 2019 EDITION

*T*HE LONG WALK HOME is a neglected classic of the escape stories born out of the mass release of Allied prisoners of war into the countryside upon Italy's surrender in September 1943. It was commissioned by the Medd family in memory of their son and completed by his escape companion Frank Simms. Its passages of incisive observation and lyrical description of landscape rank with some of the best travel writing, seasoned by a sense of being hunted, the danger of betrayal and the involuntary trust put in the help of strangers.

This new edition was inspired by and is a book of absences. Escape stories are necessarily linear; from danger to safety, from prison to freedom. The people who help, the places the escaper passes through are illumined briefly along the way then left behind. A few, a very few of them, step out from the background now to hint at their own stories and experiences as deep and dramatic as those of the protagonists.

The greatest absence in the book is Frank Simms'. Fellow escaper and second narrator, he is hardly mentioned at all in the two tributes to Peter Medd. Medd himself gives him two brief passages of praise as an inventive and witty raconteur and travelling companion. In his own completion of the story Simms' voice hardly intrudes, a marked contrast to Medd's sharp eye and sharper pen. In what we now know as an act of self-abnegation but still do not understand, Simms buried his own ambitions of being a writer to complete the Medd family's memorial to Peter.

How could a man who had a ready story or fantasy for every hour and occasion withdraw himself so utterly? Research for his Afterword in this expanded edition by Simms' son Marcus Binney has discovered in Simms a character larger, much more vital and complex; sketched from the edges in a few brushstrokes by his contemporaries and his wife but still at the centre an enigma.

The absences which inspired me to set off on this project were those of a letter from my father, now long lost, telling the story of his own escape from an Italian prison camp; the absence of my father himself, dead at 54 when I was twelve and of the stories of the Italians who literally risked life, limb and family to help. With his letter gone the only account of an experience close to his and the only book in his library on the subject, was *The Long Walk Home*. It was not until 46 years after his death that I discovered that the landscape of the Serchio valley of Medd and Simms which I had read and re-read so often was the landscape in which my father had spent ten months of 1943-44.

Discovering that landscape, I discovered the families who helped my father and indeed Medd and Simms, including surviving eyewitnesses. Researching in the myriad of individual stories of the Second War on the internet I serendipitously came across the Abrami family of London and Roggio, themselves looking for descendants of Simms and Medd and was able to bring together Marcus Binney and Frank Abrami who as a young boy had climbed a starlit mountain to bring food to the British officers in an October night of 1943. Marcus and I have tried to pay due homage to the Italians' courage by bringing this and other of their stories to the light as well.

Simms steps now out of the shadow to which his sense of duty consigned him. In addition to the character sketch in Marcus Binney's Afterword and two of his wartime poems, we include in this edition Simms' own account of the escape tunnel at the prison camp of Padula in Southern Italy, a tale and a tunnel to rival those of *The Great Escape* and the Wooden Horse.

*Andrew Adams*
*April 2019*

### Acknowledgements

As well as Frank and Mario Abrami, I would like to thank Silvia Angelini and Stefano Bucciarelli of the Istituto Storico della Resistenza e dell'Eta Contemporanea, Lucca, as well as the Banca di Memoria di Garfagnana for helping to flesh out the stories of those who helped Medd and Simms. I would also like to thank David Baynham of the Royal Regiment of Fusiliers Museum and Mike Grainger.

# FOREWORD TO THE 1951 EDITION

A FEW NIGHTS AGO, while rummaging through a stack of old manuscripts and other relics of the past, I came across a notebook in which I had once jotted down my personal and frank opinion about the fifty cadets in the Anson Term.

It is almost exactly twenty years since I was their Term Officer at Dartmouth, so you can imagine the interest with which I settled down to compare my opinions of the adolescent cadets of 1929 with the war-decorated commanders whom I know today.

How often I was wrong. Bad hats, for whom I had predicted no great future, had earned early 'brass hats' in later years; leading lights who had shone on the playing fields of Dartmouth had faded into obscurity in the more exacting game of life.

But fortunately—as those who knew Peter Medd in later life will bear me out—I had had my brighter moments. Against Peter's name I found written:

'I like this one a lot. Quiet and unassuming and always to the fore without ever being an 'eyeserver'. Goes flat out at everything and always ready to laugh. A certain bet for Cadet Captain here and odds on for a first-class N.O. later. Very keen on flying and have promised to roar him round the sky at the first opportunity. A few more like this in naval flying, and there'll be no holding us.'

And—thank heavens—there were a few more like Peter Medd, as the war was going to prove.

Perhaps I should explain the term 'eyeserver'. I am not sure whether it was a general term at the time or just one of my own, but as far as I was concerned it meant one who set out to catch the selector's eye. One who in a game of rugger let the rest of the scrum do the shoving while he waited for the break-away; who in the classroom seized every opportunity to ask a question; and who after working hours used the flimsiest excuse to knock at my cabin door.

Peter was never one of those. He pushed like mad in the scrum; never asked questions unless he definitely didn't understand; and was a more than welcome guest on the rare occasions when he came to me for advice.

And yet, although he never made himself conspicuous, his influence over the other cadets was quite staggering. As a Cadet Captain he never shouted, but they loved and respected him. When he won a sailing race (which he did frequently) he had the gift of giving the credit to the other members of his crew— and meaning it.

In the Anson Term band Peter and I both played the banjo, I provided the showmanship, Peter the melody.

Peter always provided the melody in everything he did. And it was invariably accompanied by a quiet dignity and superb good manners.

I notice that John Hayes says in his introduction that it was I who influenced Peter to specialise in naval aviation. On looking back now and realising that naval flying was responsible both for his long imprisonment and untimely death, I might be expected to have some regrets. Apart from the fact that I would give anything to see Peter's smiling face again, I have none. He volunteered for the youngest and most exciting branch of naval warfare with his eyes wide open and revelled in the thrill of speed amongst the clouds just as much as he adored the quiet of the countryside below. He was only to be allowed a short span, but he got the very utmost out of it.

In one of our last conversations Peter was bubbling over with enthusiasm about a scheme for interesting schoolboys in naval aviation. Unfortunately he was not to be spared to put his scheme into practice, but I trust that this book will in some way make amends by being widely read by the younger generation of today. They will find a fascinating story written in simple but moving language by one who loved life and was acutely conscious of the beauties around him. They will find the delight of Peter's personality in every page.

So if it encourages but a few adventurous spirits to follow in his footsteps, this book will have achieved what he would have longed for above all else.

As I said of Peter twenty years ago:

'A few more like this in naval flying, and there'll be no holding us.'

*Captain Anthony Kimmins, O.B.E., R.N. (Retd.)*

# PETER MEDD

JUST OVER TWENTY-THREE YEARS AGO fifty small boys, in uniform for the first time, panted up the hillside from the River Dart to the Royal Naval College. They were making their first bow to a life of their choice, ardent even at thirteen; and they walked too fast either to be comfortable or sensible. If it had to be a spartan life they would treat it as such from the outset.

Among them was Peter Medd and those others of us who were in time to become numbered among his nearest friends, not only because we followed the same profession, but because each of us, in one sphere or another, was to come to appreciate something of the enthusiasm which Peter radiated and to love him for the zest he gave to life in such a diversity of ways.

I must make clear from the outset the impertinence I feel in presuming to write this personal note about Peter as an introduction to his last work. There are countless people who loved him as I did and who were, I am sure, able to share more of his life. Yet there was so much to be shared with Peter that it would have been scarcely possible for any one of his friends to achieve it all. Games, sailing, languages, literature, music, ski-ing, climbing; and with it all not only was he a brilliant young leader and seaman in his Service but exceptional in the branch in which he chose to specialise, the Fleet Air Arm (as it was then called).

At college he excelled, as, I understand, he excelled at the Dragon School beforehand. His even temper, his utter lack of self-consciousness with all alike, his selflessness, his humour, his wide open honesty endeared him to all who knew him. He played all games well and sailed a boat as though born to it. He was promoted to Cadet Captain as soon as was possible and was scholastically among the leaders of his Term. There was not one of us who did not admire and respect him.

Passing out of Dartmouth with a brilliant record, he joined HMS *Rodney* in 1930 and remained in her throughout his three years as a Midshipman. He was as successful in this part of his training as his college days would lead one to expect.

Following this he embarked, with the rest of our batch, upon the round of Sub-Lieutenant's technical courses at Greenwich and Portsmouth; and it was at this time that I began to appreciate the scope of Peter's personality.

My own parents were living in Switzerland and I had not therefore the same assured escape at weekends as had my messmates. Peter noticed this and used regularly to invite me to his home in Surrey. This kindness was typical of him, for we had so far discovered very little in common. Whereas he had led in every sphere of activity at Dartmouth, my own performance had been entirely mediocre. Inspired by Anthony Kimmins, our Term Officer throughout our last two years at college and himself a pioneer of naval flying, Peter was always fascinated by this branch of the Service; my own interests were quite different; but he saw I was at a loose end and so he took me in.

Henceforth our friendship was firm. We were at the age of discovery. So much of our earliest life had been occupied by the concentrated shaping to the gunroom mould that now, with more latitude of choice in our own pursuits, our individual horizons were given their chance to extend. Although our particular interests had hitherto scarcely overlapped, we now developed an understanding, born of a mutual love of country and all that that implies.

It was, I remember, on the occasion of the birthday of His Majesty in 1934 that we were granted a long weekend from the Gunnery School. Peter and I decided to cross the spine of the South Downs from Cocking to Eastbourne. We carried packs which were foolishly heavy for the sixty miles we covered in the three days and, out of training as we were, we suffered for our folly. But on the roof of the South Coast I first knew Peter. His marked perception of detail, his buoyancy, his very love of living, his instinctive leadership to which one could not but gladly submit, combined to make him the incomparable guide and companion who was one day to prove supreme *in extremis*.

During our next leave we stayed with my parents in Switzerland. Peter loved mountains with his whole being, a love which upheld him through the complexities of his last big walk. The spirit of the hills and the dignity of high places were absorbed by him to the full, and their repose became a part of him.

I have stressed this particular side of Peter's character not because it was the side in which I could personally share most intimately, but in order to illustrate his mental approach to the escape through the mountains of Italy ten years later. Adventure he courted, risk he accepted, anxiety he concealed; so that when, in a London club, we first met after his three years of captivity he was being perfectly natural when he said: 'It was a wonderful walk, John. Just the sort you would have loved.'

The war overtook us when we were twenty-six, a little more than half-way through our Lieutenants' time. Peter had by then been in the Air Arm for five years and had already established his reputation as a pilot of courage, judgment and initiative. After serving for three years on the China Station in HMS *Eagle,* he was appointed to HMS *Warspite* in 1940. It was while carrying out reconnaissance work for that famous ship in the Mediterranean, in August of that year, that his plane was shot down and, after many hours in a rubber dinghy, he and his observer were taken prisoner by the Italians.

It is not hard to imagine what captivity must have meant to someone of Peter's outlook, particularly in those desperate early days of the war. He could have had no illusions as to the time his wings must be clipped.

They took him to an old monastery near Sulmona. As well as constantly planning to escape (which he sporadically succeeded in doing only to suffer the inevitable consequence of solitary confinement), he quickly taught himself the language of the country, an asset which was to stand him in such stead during his escape. His vivid letters, brief as they had to be, showed that his humour and his ingenuity were still sustaining him. He knew well enough where the true heart of Italy lay—among the blue-dungareed peasants who work her olive groves in an aura of garlic and strong cheroot. He found it hard to take his Fascist guards seriously.

But they were weary years for him. He was moved from camp to camp. They were moving him again, this time to Germany after Italy had capitulated, when, on the moonlit night of 13th September 1943, he saw his chance and jumped for it. That was about thirty miles north-west of Genoa.

Then followed the adventure which is told in *The Long Walk Home,* the greater part of which Peter shared with Frank Simms, a major in the Royal Warwickshire Regiment, who was playing the same critical game. Feeling for each foothold of shelter before daring to reveal their identity, existing on the country as best they could, they traversed Tuscany, Umbria, Abruzzi, with the Appenines their main protection, to reach the Allied line across the Sangro river after seven hundred miles on foot in seven weeks.

From Bari Peter came straight home and into hospital. On a grey November evening in 1943 my wife greeted me with 'Peter's home' and I felt as though the sun had come out.

As soon as he left hospital the meeting which I have already mentioned took place. The same Peter; modest, gentle, exuberant, far more anxious to hear about his godson (our son) than to talk of his adventures.

That was to be the last time I saw Peter. Once more throwing himself with zest into flying, amid the company of old friends, he began to recapture his technique. At the beginning of 1944 he was posted to a Royal Naval Air Station as C.O. of a squadron and instructor. While he was directing night landings from the ground, a pupil made a 'flat landing', the propeller flew off, hit Peter and broke his leg. This meant three more weeks in hospital and it was now that he began to develop his story from the brief notes which he had jotted down at the end of his escape. He had only half completed it when, fit enough to fly once more, he crashed with his plane through the mist into a Northumberland hillside on 19th August 1944 and was killed.

Such examples as Peter's perhaps shine the more brightly before us by the shortened span permitted them. Certainly during his few years of manhood Peter shed more happiness about him than many longer lives could justly boast.

His life was gentle; and the elements
So mixed in him, that Nature might stand up
And say to all the world, 'This was a man'.

Peter Medd was awarded the MBE early in 1944 for courage, enterprise, and devotion to duty.

When he was killed he had, as I have said, only half completed the story of his escape. The latter part remained, unembroidered and in the briefest note form, a few lines scribbled from memory during his rapid journey home from Italy.

To publish these skeleton notes would admittedly have shown the extraordinary clarity with which every incident, each personality, the slightest turn of shade and colour in the changing landscape of his wanderings must have imprinted themselves at the time on Peter's mind. It would have shown, moreover, with what twist of humour and sense of atmosphere, overlaid by resolute faith and shrewd philosophy, he was able to expand his one-word reminders into description down to the smallest detail; but at the same time, had these notes been the only way of ending the story, one would inevitably have been tantalised by conjecture of what Peter would have made of them had his life been spared.

We are therefore most fortunate in that his companion, Major Simms, possessed the same faculty for memorising detail and was consequently able to reconstruct his own narrative of the escape journey. We owe it to him, and his kindness in allowing parts of his own diary to be used, that the story did not have to be cut short. Written quite independently of each other, the two styles inevitably contrast to accent different aspects of a vagabond existence throughout those testing weeks. But the facts speak for themselves. Peter Medd and Frank Simms together formed the perfect team, each drawing upon his particular qualities in order to survive a form of ordeal which, however resolutely it may have been faced by others, can surely not have been more vividly recorded?

Of Peter, Major Simms writes:

'I would never have got through alone and I could never have had a more reliable or uncomplaining companion. Even when he had boils and his feet were bad, and his stomach gave him pain, he never grumbled. He was filled with a firm, unwavering courage of a very enduring kind, and a great and sincere belief in the principles of his country and the Navy. I will always remember him with gratitude.'

*Commander J. O. C. Hayes, O.B.E., R.N.*

# AUTHOR'S NOTE

AFTER the armistice with Italy, some twenty thousand out of the hundred thousand British prisoners in the country were free, the remainder were taken to Germany. Many of these escaped or liberated prisoners eventually reached the British lines, after innumerable adventures and hardships. Others found temporary haven in the country, fed and cared for by the peasants and working on the land in return, while they waited for the Allies to advance; and still others, through carelessness or bad luck, were rounded up by the Germans and taken away to a second grimmer captivity.

This is the story of two of the fortunate ones who got through. Our forty-eight-day trip was relatively uneventful—I have since met others whose amazing adventures make ours look like a Sunday-school outing—but it represents perhaps the average trip of the average prisoner; and as we covered a greater distance and could speak the language, we were probably better able to understand the Italian point of view than most.

Yet it is, I'm afraid, but a tenuous impression, blurred by fatigue, and sweat, and anxiety, and the hot pain of falling arches, and the impossibility of taking written notes. For most of our ten-hour day our eyes were on the ground, seeking a firm foothold for the next step. In the evening our bodies were too tired for our minds to be receptive. Certain impressions stand out: the flame of a beech tree against blue sky; white cloud frothing over a mountain top; cobwebs in frosty sunshine—but mostly they are sound impressions, for our ears were continuously straining for sounds of danger. We learnt that the harsh staccato shout of the peasant was directed at his oxen, not at us. We grew to love the whistle of the shepherds, for they were our best friends. We learnt the noises which make a mule go, and a bullock stop, and a herd of pigs come scampering to be fed. We knew the friendly sound of woodcutters at work, the thrilling whirr of partridges. And we experienced that particularly unpleasant voice used by a Fascist on the warpath.

Inevitably, one grasped something of the Italian point of view. We enjoyed their unbounded hospitality. Their industry, their simplicity, their power of self-deception, their sympathy and their lack of guts were apparent in every contact with them. (I speak, of course, of the peasant point of view—we never entered a town—but it is the peasants who are the backbone of the country—they are the real Italy.)

So I have thought it worthwhile to record this great pilgrimage of British prisoners of war, and the picture of a country facing disintegration—a country which knows it is beaten, but is quite unable to realise that it is all its own fault.

# PART ONE

*By Peter Medd*

The Route of the Escape through Italy

0   50 MILES

Turin

MILAN

MEDD JUMPED TRAIN

Alessandria

Acqui

LIGURIA

7TH DAY JOINED BY SIMMS

Genoa

EMILIA

Spezia

Corte

14TH–21ST DAY AT ROGGIO

Lucca

Pistoia

Florence

TUSCANY

27TH DAY END OF MEDD'S OWN STORY

Rimini

31ST DAY

MARCHE

Ancona

UMBRIA

Sibillini Mts.

38TH DAY

Ascoli

Gran Sasso

ROME

ABRUZZI

Pescara

43RD DAY

R. Sangro

46TH DAY

R. Trigno

47TH DAY

R. Biferno

48TH DAY REACHED BRITISH LINES

Campobasso

CAMPAGNA

Foggia

NAPLES

APULIA

Bari

LUCANIA

ARMISTICE! We heard the news at eight o'clock on the evening of 9th September. Down below, outside our small barred mess windows, there was an excited twittering from the Italian guards, cries of 'A casa!', gestures of contempt for everything military. There were soberer feelings among the prisoners: feelings of relief that a long weary chapter had come to an end; feelings of expectancy, uncertainty, the realisation that now we must think for ourselves again, and perhaps think quickly. There was no wild celebration—the vino had run out.

Our commandant, Giuseppe Moscatelli, known not the least bit affectionately to his charges as 'Joe Grapes', had lived up to his reputation and left the camp in this important hour. We were in the hands of that incompetent pair of old dugouts, de Cesare and Odino, who refused to take any action until their colonel returned.

At seven o'clock next morning we were startled by a burst of tommy-gun fire and the boom of a grenade—Germans. Soon, a very demoralised Italian ration party returned to the camp bearing the corpse of one of their number. Jerry had done his job well, posting machine guns to cover the fortress before dawn, and now, truly appreciating the Italian character, striking terror and demoralisation by one quick act of brutality. The rest was easy. Joe Grapes handed over the entire camp, lock, stock and barrel, to a German NCO and sixty men. Gavi Castle, true to its thousand-year-old tradition, had once more surrendered without a fight.

Followed four days of feverish thought and activity. We had been unable (except once) to find a way out; now one *must* be found in a hurry. A tunnel was started, to join a secret passage of which we had been told by a carabiniere. The diggers worked long hours desperately and promised us success. The tension was appalling: would it be finished before they took us away?

The diggers forecast success for Monday night, 13th September. Our hopes ran high; we began to think of 'outside' instead of 'how to get outside'. Then came the bombshell. At ten o'clock on Monday morning it was announced that all officers would leave the camp in one hour's time. This possibility had, of course, been foreseen, and hiding-places had been arranged for a certain number of us, in the hope that after we had left the Germans would evacuate the camp themselves. I had been allocated a bunk-hole, but at the last moment it seemed to me that this was merely walking into a trap: there was no other exit, and the Germans, being in no hurry, would be quite prepared to wait and starve us out; but about fifty others hid up—too many, for Jerry was bound to notice the absence of that number.

And so the forlorn remnant left Gavi for ever, more miserable even than when we had arrived at this gloomy fortress, struggling down the hill with the fraction of our accumulated possessions that it was possible or permissible to take. Past the great sunflowers, whose heads seemed turned in shame, past the Italian officers' mess, where a little group of quislings gazed at us dispassionately, down the dusty winding road to a line of commandeered buses and trucks heading, strangely, towards France.

Now, for the first time, our captors realised that we were not all there, for the special seat reserved for the brigadier remained empty. A storm burst, which, for volume of noise and confusion, rivalled anything produced by Italians. It was four hours before the convoy left for Acqui, each lorry guarded by three tommy-gunners and loaded with prisoners keyed to hair-trigger readiness to escape at the slightest opportunity, with a desperation which overcame all fear.

The greatest bogey to spontaneous escape is apathy. A fleeting opportunity occurs; you say to yourself: 'No, a better opportunity is bound to occur soon.' Or you suddenly think of the danger to the others, and, thinking, the chance slips by, never to return. You know you are determined to escape, but the starting friction is terribly hard to overcome. The secret of spontaneous escape is: Don't think—go.

On this long, uncomfortable truck ride two successful breaks were made, simultaneously. The trucks were going slowly up a winding hill, with a wooded downslope on the left, when Frank Simms and Pitchford jumped. There was no shooting: the dusty tommy-guns had jammed. For minutes there was no panic—the guards were bewildered. Then, of course, hell was let loose.

At Acqui we entrained, but there was a wait in the station for four hours before we left. During this time we were allowed to stroll on the platform. Tommy MacPherson made a daring dash for the road, and a shooting match started in the centre of the town, ending with his recapture. Two months later I found Tommy had beaten me to England, having escaped in Germany and into Sweden. No prisoner more deserved success, for his mind was passionately concentrated on thoughts of escape.

By now I was getting more desperate than ever, saying to myself that I *must* go, to justify my decision not to hide up, thinking back on three monotonous years, and forward to an unknown number of even more monotonous ones. But no opportunity seemed to come my way. Then, just before the train left, twelve of us were moved to a cattle truck near the back and locked in without guards. This truck had a sort of sentry-box sticking up in the roof, with a window for the guard to look along the top. It seemed almost too good to be true.

We left Acqui at ten-thirty in the evening. Now we had to move fast, for at Alessandria, in half an hour, we had to change trains. Quickly Captain Liebenberg, U.D.F., and I broke the sentry-box window, squeezed through and climbed down on to the buffers, he on the left side, I on the right. There we clung, waiting for the train to slow down, with a thrilling warm wind in our faces, and a wide moonlit countryside rushing by, and an overflowing feeling of freedom and happiness in our hearts. Then: 'Jump!' shouted Lieby, and I jumped.

I landed on hands and knees, and didn't even roll over—didn't even hurt myself. In a flash all my inhibitions about the risks of train-jumping dissolved. We were passing through a cutting, and the bank on my side was too high to climb, so I lay alongside the rail, under the running-board, and prayed that no inquisitive sentry would notice me as the last half of the train rumbled by. Then suddenly I found myself alone in the moonlight, with the train's red tail-light quickly receding, and not a sign of Lieby. I climbed the other bank and set off rather aimlessly across the fields, my one idea being to get away from the railway. My sense of freedom was overlaid with a feeling of loneliness and bewilderment. Here was I, alone in the great open world for the first time in three years, dressed only in check shirt, plus-fours, stockings and shoes, my only possessions a tin of Ovaltine tablets and one hundred lire, for in the last-minute excitement my well-prepared escape outfit was forgotten. Here was no comforting routine, no certainty, no solid foundation of prison camp life to drug my senses. Now I must think, and act, and make decisions. The responsibility seemed overpowering.

So I walked to a farmhouse, told them how I had escaped, and asked for help. What a friendly welcome for a refugee! I was pressed into a chair, given bread and cheese and wine, surrounded by a crowd of inquisitive and excited people. Here was the padrone of the house and his family, and charming Mariuccia Pesca and her sister, evacuated from Genoa—the first girls I had been face to face with for three years—and one of their male admirers from a neighbouring house.

We talked of escape, and Germans, and Mussolini, and my plans. They were pathetically optimistic: the British would land at Genoa in a few days, and my best plan was to get into 'plainer' clothes and remain hidden in the district until rescued. I accepted, at least, the offer of plain clothes, and Mariuccia's boy friend took me to his house to get them.

There, his pretty young sister came down in her nightdress and found me more bread and cheese and wine, while I changed my too-English clothes for worn black coat and trousers, a blue shirt and Trilby hat. Then I left them: wished on my way by whispered 'auguri' and bits of advice, touched and encouraged by such spontaneous generosity. Living in Italy as a refugee was not going to be so hard, after all.

I wandered up into the hills left of Acqui, revelling in the warm night, the full moon, the wide space and freedom. At last I made myself a bed in the bracken in a small coppice and fell asleep to the murmur of strange forgotten sounds—wind rustling through trees, an owl hooting, the distant bark of a watchdog. It was hard to distinguish where reality ended and dreams began. I half expected to see Titania appear.

### Second Day
THE SUN woke me, flickering through the leaves, casting long shadows across the bracken, stirring into life suspicious black-birds and inquisitive lizards, and industrious spiders who seemed intent on binding me to my brackeny couch.

I climbed to the top of the hill, where the wood ended, and vineyards began, with widely spaced farmhouses, still asleep. To the south-east the slope dropped steeply to the Alessandria-Acqui valley, containing the main road, railway and river, with, beyond, a jumble of hills fading to the faint outline of the Gavi mountains. To the south lay the main range of the Apennines, higher and more wild, stretching away to France. To the north the ground sloped down to the broad Po valley, with, beyond, a suspicion of Alps, the great massif of Mont Blanc and Monte Rosa.

So I lay there till noon among the vines, feeding myself on fat red and white grapes, sweating slightly as the hot sun rose in a cloudless sky, watching the endless German convoys going south along the road, and trying to decide on a plan.

There were three choices; I might go to France. It was only fifty miles away, and the German guards had told us a landing had been made at Toulon. If not, one could probably get to Spain, but that would be a long way, and I couldn't be certain of help from the French. Or I might go to Switzerland. This was close, too—just eighty miles across the plain—but we had heard the Germans and Swiss were guarding the two sides of the frontier, and, anyway, once there, would one ever get out? Unlimited winter sports would be magnificent, but it wasn't war. Finally, there was the walk down through Italy to join our advancing army. With luck, they would do most of the walking. Little did I guess how wrong I was!

So I chose the third, but first I decided to go back to Gavi. The Germans might have evacuated it, and the boys hiding up might want the tip to come out. Then, David Stirling, one of the hidden, had selected a commando team, in which I was to practise guerilla tactics in northern Italy. There might still be a chance of joining up and having our fun.

About noon I descended the hill, crossed the main road in a lull between convoys, and headed through the maize fields for the river, sheathed in its coat of tall poplars and thick undergrowth. There I found a ford, where the swift knee-deep water rushed in foam over the tumbled rocks, and waded across, feeling rather ridiculous under the placid stare of a couple of sleek white oxen.

Soon I reached a road again, and here I got my first fright. A sinister little man in a black hat—the swarthy aquiline type of Italian—said to me: 'Dove andala?' ('Where are you going?') in that unpleasant tone of voice I had already learnt to associate with Fascists and Carabinieri. I mumbled an unconvincing reply and hurried on as fast as I could with dignity, heading for the hills.

There on the hillside I found a white house, with a white-haired old man mending a wine cask outside the front door. I told him I was an escaped British prisoner and asked for help. He looked up fiercely. 'How do you know I am not a Fascist?' Then his blue eyes twinkled.

He was a retired merchant skipper, evacuated here from Genoa, with his family. We went indoors and met his wife, thin and frail, and utterly worn out with years of too much work. This family—there was a daughter, too—was living on the starvation line. They had nothing, absolutely nothing. The neighbouring farmers charged them fantastic prices for food, or refused to sell, so they lived on the ration, which was inadequate and not always obtainable nowadays. Their Genoa home had been bombed, and here they lived in this empty house with a few salved bits of furniture and bedding. They suffered in silence. Her sympathy was all for me, a 'poverino' who couldn't go home, and he never talked about hardships except to say gruffly that it was all their own fault for ever having put up with Mussolini. In this he was the most enlightened Italian I ever met.

The day faded. Mrs Valente set about preparing the supper, and we went out on to the flat roof and looked at the landscape through a pair of ancient binoculars, the sort that every retired old sailor has, which shows two images and is unadjustable. There we talked of the sea, dispassionately, for he showed no feelings of any sort. Yet I think he was glad to be able to talk once more with another sailor. Then we went in to supper.

Polenta—the staple dish of the poor in northern Italy—tomatoes and walnuts. This is what they lived on. She apologised continually: he grunted and said nothing. After supper the daughter arrived, bringing a breath of fresh air into this rather embarrassing atmosphere. She worked in an office in Genoa:

left home on foot at four-thirty every morning on a two-hour walk to the station. (You daren't bicycle these days: the thing would be stolen within twenty-four hours.) Then a two-and-a-half-hour ride in a cattle truck, owing to the shortage of rolling stock, would get her to the office about nine. There she worked until four-thirty in the afternoon, when the long ride home began.

In spite of a sixteen-and-a-half-hour day, she had a freshness and gaiety about her which was charming. As she described her day, there was never a hint of hardship or overwork. Her Italian accent would have penetrated an air-raid shelter; her Genoese dialect was quite incomprehensible. She had brought back the week's ration of flour, sugar, and salt. Each pathetic little package was unwrapped with the excitement of a child over a Christmas stocking. We all went to bed early, for tomorrow morning we must get up at four. I had a mattress on the floor of the old man's bedroom and slept like a log.

### Third Day

THE ALARM clock woke us punctually, and we breakfasted off hot milk and stale bread in the pungent light of an acetylene lamp. Mrs Valente, her daughter, and I left the house at four-thirty for the long walk to the station. I don't know whether the chaperoning was on account of me: the old woman excused herself by saying she made the trip every day.

My way lay eastwards towards Ovada, so I left them short of the station and set off along the road in the pale dawn light. For the first half-hour I met nobody, but then the countryside began to wake up. Sleepy bullock carts rumbled by, the fields seemed imperceptibly to sprout with peasants engaged in the eternal task of hoeing. I was glad to find I raised no curiosity in them. But as the morning activity increased I decided to leave the road—it was the sight of a German ambulance parked by the kerb just ahead which finally decided me—and travelled eastwards across a country of steep hills and gullies, vineyards on the slopes and thick undergrowth in the hollows. My lunch was a handful of walnuts and some stolen grapes, eaten in the sunshine in the dry bed of a stream.

About noon I reached Ovada. Here, I remembered, was a German headquarters; the place had been stiff with troops when we came through three days before. I sneaked across the main road, and under the railway by a culvert, and so up into the wooded hills to the south. This was not the most direct way to Gavi, but I wanted to reach the main west-east ridge of the mountains, where going would be easier and safer than among the foothills, with their criss-cross system of rivers, roads, and railways.

By now the sun had vanished in a white haze, which darkened and condensed to torrential rain. Even this did not lessen my unaccustomed joy of freedom. There were more pleasures to be rediscovered among these woods: the intoxicating scent of damp pine needles, the sight of bright-eyed little birds hopping silently through the undergrowth, the sudden explosion of disturbed partridges taking to the air, or of a startled hare zigzagging across the hillside. These were strange, exciting sensations for me, and I thought to myself, in the old familiar words: 'Ain't nature wonderful?' It was not until days later that I realised the absolute paucity of wild life in Italy. A similar countryside of woods and mountains in England would teem with life, yet here in Italy one sometimes walked a whole day without seeing flesh or fowl, save the vulgar crow wheeling overhead, and lizards and snakes scuttling for cover. I never saw a rabbit in Italy, except a tame one. There were a few hares and partridges, fewer squirrels and pheasants. Even the small bird life is practically non-existent. For every Italian countryman carries a shotgun, and anything over the size of a sparrow is fair game to him. There are laws, indeed—shooting begins officially on 1st October—but all laws, the Italian believes, are made to be broken. This year the German requisitioning of all firearms will probably give Italian wildlife such a chance as it has never had before, though even this order, carrying the death sentence as penalty for disobedience, is only being partly carried out.

Up there, in the mist and woods, I lost my sense of direction, so decided to go down and take shelter in a farmhouse. I found one in a fold of the hill, almost overgrown by the wood, attached to a tiny vegetable garden and vineyard, which seemed the only means of support for the swarm of dirty children and old women who filled the single ground room. Here they gave me bread and wine, and gazed at me in wonder, tremendously intrigued to meet an Englishman for the first time. Then, the rain stopping, a small child guided me down to the river and across the Ovada-Genoa railway, and left me to climb into the oak woods on the other side, north-eastwards towards Gavi.

A quarter of an hour later, passing a farmhouse, an old man came out and called: 'Come in, giovanotto, and have a drink.' I refused, for it was getting late and I had far to go, but he insisted. His son, he said, had just reached home from France, where he and his fellow soldiers had been ordered to lay down their arms after the armistice. When I admitted I was English, the soldier turned to me and said earnestly: 'Never tell that to anyone. The country is full of Fascist spies. Say you are a soldier of the Italian 4th Army, disbanded in Toulon, returning to your home in Trieste. Your accent will pass for a Triestino in this part of the country.'

This was interesting. I hadn't realised till then that Italy is such a honeycomb of self-contained cells, each having its own customs and speaking its own dialect, that country people are easily fooled by the accent of a 'foreigner' from a different part of the country.

Shortly afterwards, on the road to Gavi, I had an opportunity of trying this out. An old peasant attached himself to me, and we walked together for five miles, discussing every sort of subject, and to the end he believed me a good Triestino who had laid down his arms in the service of his country, and was now going to the only sensible place for an Italian—home.

This road led us along the crest of a tortuous range of hills, scarred by deep eroded gullies and cut by streams. Here and there in this desolate landscape were fantastic villages, perched on the very tops of rocky pinnacles, secure from the invader of olden days who ravaged their vineyards and fields on the lower slopes.

The rain had cleared and left a fine, steamy-blue evening. The old familiar Gavi landmarks drew slowly closer. The peasants were going home, many of them heading for their nearest village, taking their firearms to be handed in to the German command, or local podista. One man passed us, almost hysterical with anger, waving a big .45 revolver, and crying that he had tried to hide it, but had been denounced.

At last Gavi Monastery came in sight, winking like a lighthouse in the setting sun. I climbed its winding ramp in the dusk, considerably excited at seeking refuge so near to the lion's den.

After the armistice, our Italian chaplain had told us that, in the event of escape, we could safely ask for help at any monastery, and that he would warn Gavi Monastery to expect refugees. I didn't know who to ask for or where to go, and before I knew where I was found myself face to face with a white-coifed nun. I asked for the priests' quarters and foolishly told her that I was an escaped British prisoner—so soon had I forgotten the soldier's advice. In a moment the news had reached all the women, and even the children in the attached orphanage heard about it and came to peer at me round corners.

Then I met the Father. He led me to the ramparts and looked at me a long time without saying a word. Then: 'Are you a Catholic?' he asked. No, a Protestant, I confessed, and felt for a moment that I was going to be turned shamefully away, an infidel and outcast. 'Never mind,' he said, 'we offer shelter to everybody.' We stood in silence gazing across the valley to where Gavi Castle reared its gloomy shadow out of the mist, the very embodiment of all that is evil and sinister. The arc lights glinted balefully: so the Germans were still in occupation. I thought miserably of those unfortunate fellows who lay hidden there, walled up in cold, dank holes, unable to talk or light a match, or move about, wondering whether Jerry was still there or not, wondering whether the next moment would bring a hand grenade bouncing down on them. And I was very glad of my decision not to hide up.

The Father was talking in a low, precise voice. It was a reprimand to me for spreading the news that I was English. 'Those women cannot hold their tongues. Already the news may be down in the village. The Church is always suspect, and we are closely watched here.'

I was beginning to be quite windy. But that was nothing to what was to come. I was told to hide in the garden while he removed the watchdog from the side door. Then we crept quickly in on tiptoe, up the stairs to his room, and locked ourselves in. Soon there was a knock at the door. 'Who is it?' asked the priest, and there was a mumbled reply from outside. 'Well, you can't come in now, I am busy,' said the priest in a tone of voice which would have raised curiosity and excitement in the dumbest listener. If there were any who hadn't heard of my arrival from the nun, they would soon learn now that there were strange goings-on in Gavi Monastery that night.

When the steps had died away, he led me on an inspection of the boltholes. 'You see,' he said, 'we have two exits from this place. If they come by this door, you creep down the stairs, through the vestry and out the back. If they come by the back door, I'll keep them talking until you can get out the side door. And just to be quite certain, we'll hang this rope out of the pantry window, and you can climb down that.'

By this time I was thoroughly jittery, seeing a German round every corner. Then suddenly I realised that this good man was enjoying himself as never before. The traditional monastic spirit of intrigue flowed in his veins. This promised to be the best thing that had happened in Gavi since the days of the Borgia Pope. I laughed to myself and went up to enjoy my supper with a quiet heart.

I fed alone—steaming ministra, bread, cheese and wine—watched by the Father and another priest. They told me the Germans showed no signs of leaving the castle, but so far had caught no prisoners. We talked little, for I was very tired.

The Father's quarters consisted of a sitting-room, bedroom, and pantry. The inside wall of the sitting-room had a window giving out into the chapel. In this room they made me up a bed on a couch; spring mattress and clean sheets, and two pillows. As I slipped into this heaven of softness, a boy started to play the organ, slow quiet chords. The dangers of life seemed infinitely remote. I went to sleep with the peace of mind of the mediaeval refugee who sought sanctuary at the altar and knew he was safe. Even the rope in the pantry window couldn't keep me awake.

### Fourth Day

THE GOOD Father woke me at four-thirty, and I think he was disappointed the night had been so uneventful. While I ate my bread-and-wine breakfast, he gave me his advice. He suggested I go and call on the parish priest of a nearby village, Alice. 'He is a well-informed man, who knows the country and always listens to the English broadcasts.'

I slipped down the hill in the half light, before the inquisitive nuns were awake, and took the road eastwards to Alice. Away over on the left was the sombre fortress of Gavi, brooding over its secrets. Neither hill nor wood seemed to hide me from the baleful stare of those arc lights.

The sun was up when I reached Alice, and Mass was about to begin as I entered the vestry and introduced myself to the 'parocco'. He was fat and genial, his face full of an owlish wisdom, and his eyes twinkled as he heard my story. He thought for a while, suggested a course of action at great length, cancelled it, and thought again. From time to time a black-veiled woman would come in and urge him to begin the Mass, but his mind was on more worldly matters now. Then he began talking again. It was his opinion, too, that I should stay round here and wait for a nearby landing, and he suggested the name of a family, who lived way up in the hills, who would look after me or pass me on to their relations. I decided to go there: perhaps it would be possible to get passed on from house to house, right down to the British lines? I had no faith at all in the theory of a British landing up this end of the country.

So I left him to take his Mass, and was pulled into the kitchen by his niece (the rectory, in country Italy, is attached to the church) and served with hot milk and bread. She was also an evacuee from Genoa. Her enthusiasm for Britain, and her desire to help me, were most reassuring. I began to realise that I was in a friendly country.

On I went, then, across the tiny stream in its wide bed of smooth white pebbles, where the village women were already ranged on their knees, pounding their dirty linen, and up the other bank through the vineyards to pleasant oak woods. Here was a 'riserva di caccia'—a game reserve—which seemed to contain more game than the unrestricted areas, in spite of occasional shots in the distance.

At last I found my house—the 'Casa Brucciata'—a neat clean farmhouse sitting on a green, undulating grassy alp. There was suddenly something rather Swiss about the scene, a change from the nearby oak woods.

In the doorway sat an old woman peeling potatoes. I told her of my visit to the parson and introduced myself as an escaped British prisoner. 'How can you prove it?' she said suspiciously. This was a bit difficult, because I had no identity marks. The letter addressed to me at Gavi which I had saved for this very purpose was still in my coat on the way to Germany.

'Well, I can't prove it, but I certainly am English,' and my ingenuousness must have convinced her, for she softened a bit. Then I asked her if I could stay, as the priest had said, and she was again cautious in her reply. 'You must wait until the men return. You understand, I, too, am under orders here.'

So I went out on to the grassy mountainside and slept in the sun until lunchtime. I got back to the house just as the men were coming in from work. I and my story were received gravely, but with great politeness. I could see they weren't particularly taken with the idea of putting me up, or passing me on to friends, and I wondered what my next move should be.

Lunch was now ready, and we went into the kitchen. The padrone—the old woman's husband—took the end of the table, and motioned me to a place on his right. At the other end of the table sat his two sons and a youth of about fourteen. An immense bowl of steaming minestra was placed before him, and he filled my plate and his. Then the other men helped themselves. It is delicious filling stuff, this minestra, made of macaroni, potatoes, beans, herbs, sometimes bits of meat, all mixed into the consistency of Irish stew. We had three helpings each (second and third helpings are the rule in Italy; what a pity it is considered greedy at home!). We drank water, the padrone and I having a glass each, the remainder drinking from a huge ladle, which they dipped into a central bowl. When all the men had finished eating, the minestra was removed and the women got down to their share—not much, for there wasn't much left—which they ate sitting on stools in corners, or standing. Then all the men got up and went upstairs for two hours' siesta, with never a word to me.

This was my first introduction to Italian peasant society. The feudal primitiveness of it is almost terrifying. Man is a god, the head of the family a super god. The women are servants, never speaking in the presence of men unless spoken to, never pushing themselves forward, working ceaselessly from before dawn to dusk, uncomplainingly. They know their position; it would never enter their heads to try and alter it.

The woman had told me that many Italian soldiers passed the Casa Brucciata on their way home, so I decided to await the afternoon in the sun and attach myself to any party who would have me. Living in this austere family would be impossible, I realised, and, anyway, it wouldn't help me to join up with our Army.

About three o'clock a party of five arrived at the farm, singing and chattering like a covey of magpies. They welcomed me enthusiastically. They were going to Rome, and of course I could come along with them.

We swapped stories in front of the farmhouse, while they munched the bread given them by the old woman. Then suddenly, with no apparent word of command, they were off again up the path to Rome, laughing and shouting, and I with them.

Carlo, Giuliano, Augusto, Giuseppe, and Renzo. It was Renzo Baccani who invited me to come along. He attached himself to me almost as personal bodyguard, taught me the peculiar ways of Italian soldiers, steered me through many dangers, and shared everything he possessed with me. Carlo Bergamino was our leader. He might have been the original Charlie Chaplin: the little cane, the outsize trousers, the absurd moustache. He walked in decrepit sandals. And on top of this music-hall personality he had a superb power of command, which enabled him more or less to control his irresponsible companions and to stifle at source the many embryo arguments.

We had only walked for ten minutes from the Casa Brucciata when the whole team suddenly stopped, unpacked their lunch, and settled down to a huge lunch of bread and cheese and tinned fish, in which I was compelled to join. But ten minutes later Carlo had us on the road again.

We climbed to the top of our particular mountain, from which we looked down into a deep valley, and beyond the imposing massif of the big mountain which used to dominate the Gavi landscape. Down to the right the valley led away to Voltaggio, and this was our direction.

Voltaggio presented a certain danger. We knew it to be full of Germans, yet there was no avoiding the town. But here again we were lucky. A charming Genoa evacuee attached herself to us and offered to guide us through the town by safe back streets.

On the far outskirts of the town we stopped again and said goodbye to our fair guide. An admiring crowd of spectators collected round us, and the whole story of the escape from France had to be retold.

These soldiers belonged to the 4th Italian Army, garrisoning Toulon. On the signing of the armistice the general ordered his men to lay down their arms and confined them to barracks. Followed a mass breakout by the troops, breaking down the doors with hand grenades. The fugitives took the train to Turin (still in Italian hands), where they broke up into small parties, changed into plain clothes, and started the long trek to their homes.

We were about to move on to find a lodging place for the night further from the town, when the padrone of the nearby farmhouse invited us to stay with him. We accepted. It was convenient, for here close to the farm flowed the river, and we were able to bathe and wash our clothes. Then we sat on the step in the twilight talking to our hosts, and two lovely evacuees brought us vino. They drew me aside and said: 'You are not Italian, are you? American or English?' Then one of them told me she was engaged to an Italian naval officer, Lieutenant Casinaghi, and would I please call on him when we crossed the line, for he had gone to Malta with the Italian fleet, and she had had no news of him for a long time. I realised then it was no good trying to fool an educated Italian with my accent.

I fell in love with these girls from Zena, in fact all the Genoese girls I had met. Their soft accent is delicious. They know how to make themselves attractive in a not-too-sophisticated way, in spite of the rigours of war. There is a practical good sense about them, so different from the hothouse-plant type which one associates more with this Mediterranean climate. They reminded me of the English girls of Shanghai: vivacious, hardworking, with an immense appreciation for life.

Then we had supper—a hugely amusing supper. The vino flowed, the minestra came again and again in steaming platefuls, and Carlo and Augusto kept up a cross talk—mostly in different dialects—which kept the company in fits of laughter. Augusto has one passion, catching chickens. He dreams and talks all day about catching chickens. And now he described, in brilliant fashion, his failures and successes in this line since leaving Turin.

Finally, we were shown to bed in the loft, all rather tipsy and hysterical. Life seemed good. We were free, we were going home. Soon—any day now—the British would land at Genoa, and there would be no more war, but instead unlimited food and luxuries and work for all. Poor, self-deceiving Italy!

### Fifth Day

WE WERE off at seven o'clock, up the mountain path, with ridiculous Carlo in the lead, slap-slapping his sandals, Augusto muttering about the chicken that got away, Renzo attached to me like the faithful hound. Now we encountered other parties, some going our way, some the other. We greeted each other like clipper ships passing on the distant trade routes:

'Where do you come from?'

'Toulon, 4th Army.'

'Where are you going?'

'Rome.'

'Goodbye and good luck.'

But sometimes the appearance of another party would be the excuse for a halt and a fuller exchange of stories.

'Yes. We're engineers of the Tara Division. On the armistice our general betrayed us. Made us lay down our arms and confined us to barracks. We burst the door open with a hand grenade and marched out. Took the train to Turin, then walked. Nine days…. And you?'

Then Carlo would suddenly call us to our feet with the cry of 'Duma!' (Duma—Genoese for andiamo=let's go) and shuffle off, twirling his stick, not waiting for the conversation to cease or the convoy to assemble.

Thus we spent our days together—stopping for a talk, stopping for a sudden snack of bread and cheese, stopping to pick grapes or accept a glass of wine, each time rallied again to the trail by Carlo and his 'Duma!'

All these soldiers we passed had similar stories. We in prison camps were not the only ones to suffer from the lamentable lack of initiative shown by the Italian officers. The rot started at the top. Badoglio had apparently issued no orders about action to be taken at the armistice, and his commanding generals showed an acute tendency to paralysis. Most of them did nothing until the approach of Germans revivified the sense of self-preservation in them, and they took the easiest line to save their own skins. This usually was to disarm and allow themselves to be taken prisoner. Sometimes (as in the 4th Army) they disarmed and shut themselves in before the Germans arrived, in that embarrassing way they had in East Africa. Sometimes—very occasionally—they fought, but it was only a token resistance, and collapsed as soon as the German strength reached about ten per cent of the Italian. If anyone still wanted confirmation on the Italian fighting qualities, here, in the armistice, they had it.

About noon we reached at Ronco the great rift that runs north and south through the mountains, containing the Milan-Genoa auto-strada and main road and railway. We crossed this in line ahead, at one-hundred-yard intervals, looking incredibly furtive, I thought. But luckily there were no Germans to see this quaint team tiptoeing down gullies, sprinting across open spaces, creeping under culverts, and finally disappearing into merciful cover among the hazel bushes on the eastern side. I thought of this six weeks later when Frank and I were in no-man's-land and felt glad we were not still members of that crazy gang.

Up there among the hazels we found leaflets—German leaflets dropped for the benefit of the Italians. They were all about us. The German Government would give the equivalent of twenty English pounds, plus extra rations of food and tobacco to anyone handing over to them an escaped British prisoner of war. But, on the other hand, should anyone be found guilty of helping a British POW he would be punished with the death penalty. A declaration destined to have absolutely no effect on about ninety-nine per cent of the Italian population.

We trudged on, now up hill, now down, now through thick woods and now over grassy slopes, until the orange tint in the sunlight told us it was time to find a home for the night. But just then Carlo seemed to have steered us into the most impenetrable part of the macchia. The path, which had started robustly as a mule-track, had suddenly disappeared into nothing. The briar bushes, once so neat and isolated, now trailed their thorny sinews everywhere. Even some of the trees seemed to have fallen down just to get in the way. We were trying to reach the top of a hill, where I thought I had seen a village. Now, suddenly, in face of all these difficulties, the morale of these soldiers suddenly cracked. Some said on, and some said back. Some said there wasn't a village up there at all—even Carlo seemed to have lost his power of leadership. In this moment of their distress they turned to me, being an officer, for decision. And when I, doing a mental toss-up, said 'On', they followed like lambs, while I prayed that there really was a village at the top.

There was, and we reached it quicker than any of us would have guessed. The ease with which we came out of that macchia surprised me, too, but by keeping a straight face I managed to make it look as if I'd known it all along. This brought a new respect for me and made up for my lack of all the essential qualities, like being able to sing Italian opera on the march, talk all the dialects in Italy, or tell one sort of grape from another.

This anonymous little village sat on a hilltop surrounded by its vineyards and tiny plantations and protected apparently from all contact with the world by its apron of wilderness. We found an Osteria, whose flimsy balcony almost overlapped the roof of the next house downhill. No, they couldn't give us anything to eat, or find us a 'fienile' to sleep in. Yes, they were an inn, but they didn't do that sort of thing. We could have some vino if we liked, and then the crazy gang dispersed to hunt out food and lodging for the night.

### Sixth Day

THE PLACID Swiss or Austrian builds his village in the valley, where water is plentiful and the meadows are lush, and he can look up and worship his mountain peaks. But the Italian, also peace-loving but timid, chooses the most inaccessible places he can find. His villages cling like grey bats to the rock face, or balance precariously on the very pinnacles of mountains. They are not things of beauty, but they cause a gasp of admiration at their very tenacity. The drab grey stone blends almost imperceptibly into the living rock. Approaching, you can make out the features of the houses, apparently thrown indiscriminately one on top of the other. They are so tumble-down, and there are so many unglazed windows that it is hard to tell whether they are deserted or occupied. Going closer still, you are no longer in doubt. The steep track leading up to the main street (or drain—it's the same) is churned into a quagmire by the feet of many men and women, donkeys, mules, oxen, and sheep. Perhaps near the foot of the village is the spring, spouting its super-cool mountain water into a long stone trough. This is the meeting-place for the village women. Here they wash their interminable laundry and fill their stone pitchers and iron cauldrons for cooking and washing in the home, while the local gossip in excruciating dialect is tossed about like a ping-pong ball.

The main street appears to be almost vertical. Mostly it is a muddy chute, but here and there it generously becomes a series of stone steps. Steps or chute are equally negotiable to the bare-footed water-women whose pitcher never leaves the head until it has been manœuvred under the six-foot door lintel and actually into the house. The street is dark after the hard sunlight below, for the houses each side are close, and from time to time are built right across. Under these arches, in gloomy cells, live the cattle, adding their own particular smell to the general mixed bouquet of the village. Be careful when emerging from the tunnel: you may get a bucket of slops down the back of your neck. Either side of the street are the dark entrances of houses, emitting loud children's noises, and perhaps shops, though usually you won't find more than a cobbler, a single store, and an inn in each village. And people come and go up and down the street continually: the water-women, the scampering children, men leading heavy-laden mules or ponderous oxen.

Further up, a square has somehow been conjured out of the steep hillside. Here is the podestà, the mayor's house, better built perhaps than the rest, but still looking tumbledown with all the scaffolding holes empty. The wall is decorated with the latest German notices—the handing over of British prisoners, the order for Italians of military age to present themselves for work, the rationing regulations. The German High Command orders this, the German High Command orders that. And the death penalty for everything.

Having such a podestà, this village must be a centre of a commune, the collection of tiny villages and isolated farms which forms the unit of local government. In turn the commune is responsible to the province, which is responsible to the central government. The old states—now called regions—are official anachronisms. But state loyalty runs deep in Italy and cannot be removed by a few years of Fascist legislation.

Here, too, in the square, is the church, its single huge bell never idle for long. Under its roof is also the priest's house, so that he can walk from his parlour into the vestry. And perhaps alongside the church is the school, closed now for the long summer vacation which will not end until October. In smaller villages the school will be open in the evenings as a sort of social centre, equipped with a state-provided radio. But here, in the commune, we have a fine big dopolavoro building, still showing the Duce's face and the Fasces, dimly, through the new coat of paint—still gallantly flaunting 'CREDERE, UBBEDIRE'—but the third of the trio 'COMBATTERE' has been painted out—('Believe, Obey'—'Fight'). This dopolavoro is the social centre-cum-pub of the village, and not so many days ago the propaganda centre as well.

So you reach the top of the pinnacle, and, finding a minute open space, look down on a perfect jigsaw puzzle of untidy roofs, each overlapping the next, so that from here no street is visible, and only a sort of depression in the puzzle indicates where the square is. And away down beyond the grey roofs is a riot of sunlit colour—vineyards, green meadows, waving maize, down to the deep green chestnut woods, and up again to the blue-grey mountain beyond the valley, and the intense unbroken blue of the Italian sky.

Today we moved suddenly into another landscape. Crossing a pass, we were met with the sight of grey rock precipices and immense buttresses, and a skyline of razor-edge pinnacles. And below were grassy, Alpine slopes and white, red-roofed chalets. There was more grandeur about this scenery than in the rounded slopes behind us. I felt more friendly towards it, too, for this was something I knew—Swiss scenery. These were indeed Apennines, not effeminate Ligurian Alps.

We stepped down the blue-and-white crocus carpet to the terraced vineyards. Here grew the exquisite Fragole and

Americana, huge, succulent, strawberry-flavoured grapes, delicious to eat but disappointing in wine. We reached up and plucked great bunches of them as we walked. Down below in the village we stopped for lunch. This was a much cleaner village, a red-and-white affair, and, from the style of its Osteria, it was used to summer visitors. Once more we were idolised by the villagers—gallant soldiers who had done our bit and were now going home (it was that which appealed to them: we were going home). The armistice had been signed: soon the British would land at Genoa and all would be well. Life was just a lovely holiday. Seven families bolted away and produced seven steaming plates of minestrone, which we ate on the balcony of the inn.

Here we met Alfreda Pucci, very neat and quiet, walking to Rome. He had been guard in a British POW working camp, he said, offering me a Gold Flake cigarette. They had all been the greatest of friends there, guards and prisoners, and on the armistice had agreed to liquidate the firm. So here he was, walking home, with his pockets full of Red Cross soap.

He joined the crazy gang, and we 'duma-ed' once more. Up an interminable valley, with Monte Antola on our left. Down the other slope to another muddy village, enjoying the name of Barbagelata—frozen beard. Here we sat for a rest and a drink until, in place of the usual cheery 'duma' Carlo came up and said he was leaving us, to branch off to his home at Chiaveru (he pronounced the ch soft, like cheese). Augusto, who lived at Reggio Emilia, and Giuseppe were going with him. There was a complicated exchange of addresses, and a certain amount of sentimentality, and they were gone, squelching down the muddy street on the road to the coast. I suddenly felt flat, all the character seemed to have gone out of our happy team. The carefree nonsensical atmosphere was gone, and I realised that escaping was really a stark business, not a holiday.

Thus I sat, with my chin in my hands, on the stone seat

in the village square, while the daylight faded, and the fat white cows came ambling home to bed, and Giuliano was an interminable time arranging our lodgings for the night.

## Seventh Day

DOWN the road from Barbagelata, next morning, we passed a sailor, blue trousers tucked into his boots, kitbag across his shoulder. He, too, was walking home. He told us there was an Englishman staying at the Osteria, so we decided to investigate. Our enquiry was received with suspicion by the landlady, but she went upstairs to report. Next, an anxious face appeared at an upper window, to be transformed suddenly into a broad smile of recognition. It was Frank Simms, who had escaped six hours before me from the lorry.

Here was Frank, living in luxury like any country squire. Living in inns, paying his way and actually—horror of horrors!—tipping when he left! This was not my line of country at all. I was the poor refugee, sometimes Italian, sometimes English, requesting charity. I think the peasants preferred it that way. They would have been insulted at offers of money. And, looked at more cynically, it was Badoglio's job to look after us as long as we were in the country—his fault that we we were having to do all this. I was always ready, except when posing as an Italian, to leave my name and address, so that our kind hosts could later claim compensation for helping a British POW.

But Frank is a hundred per cent British. One of those who would wear a dinner jacket in the jungle. I'm not laughing at this. Frank's fifteen years in the Colonial army in the Sudan have taught him how best to maintain British prestige among 'inferior races'. It was an admirable policy among this race of Italians, in some ways, but a little too public for safety.

I was delighted to meet such a friend as travelling companion, and Frank, who had walked alone so far, was also glad of companionship. With the unanimous and spontaneous assent of the crazy gang, he was enrolled a member, and we moved on.

It was a difficult day, amid tremendous mountain formations. The monstrous peaks, wreathed in troubled clouds, quite belied their modest five thousand feet. But, in miniature, this country had all the grandeur and the difficulties of larger mountain masses. Climbing one precipitous, boulder-strewn pass merely brought you face to face with another deep valley, scarred with gorges and white-fanged torrents, tumbling down to the main stream. It was an utterly desolate scene. Towards evening we found ourselves high on the mountain side below the Cento Croce, and here we decided to stay the night in the miniature village of Sopra la Chicoa. Sopra la Chicoa only had five houses, all desperately poor, so that once more it meant dispersing ourselves among them for the evening meal. Our reception here was even more hospitable than usual, confirming a growing conviction that the poorer the family, the kinder they were.

Renzo and I supped at the house of a blue-eyed peasant woman of about forty. Her vivacity quite overcame the appearance of drudgery and premature old-age which most of these people have, and the disfigurement of a goitre, which also is common in these northern mountains. We fed off an immense minestrone. Three plateloads of it induced a state of perfect nirvana, a sleep-inducing inward glow. We were very content.

### Eighth Day

IT IS Monday, 20th September. We have had a week of liberty. I wonder about the others hiding in the Fortress at Gavi—by now their food must have run out, and they will have had to give themselves up. (Six weeks later, in England, I heard they had all been recaptured.)

Giuliano is now our leader, and a very bad one. He seems to have no idea of direction. The sun, to him, might just as well be going north-about. And, besides, he is temperamental. One moment he will rush ahead, neglecting the less agile members of his team, then, remembering them suddenly, will stop and pour abuse at them. Or, having led us into an inextricably wrong hole, he will lose heart and sulk, and somebody else has to solve the problem for him.

By now my old shoes are in a most disreputable state. The soles have worn right off both of them, and to save my stockings I have tied sacking round the derelict uppers. But it keeps on slipping off or wearing through, and is a perpetual nuisance; we tried to get them repaired in a village, but the cobbler said they had gone too far.

Towards evening we entered a land of rolling hills, chestnut covered. The deep, luxuriant green foreground paled into a blue-grey distance, wave after wave of finely shaded hills, like a limitless ocean, with the sun setting in it from a cloudless sky. Up on the shoulder of one of these billows we found a small village, red roofs and white walls, and a tall campanile. Evacuees were arriving, their trunks and furniture piled on mules, and the local doctor was returning on horseback from his far-flung round.

We found a small house to stay in, where Giuliano discovered an old army friend. It was decided that Frank should remain silent, so that we could all pass as Italians. Our host, halfway through supper, did remark that one of our number seemed very quiet, but we passed it off, saying he was tired. Later, Frank went outside and a moment later we heard a faint cry from him. Giuliano went out to investigate and found poor Frank had fallen into the cesspit, almost up to the waist! On to this appalling scene came the padrone, and Frank couldn't very well maintain his silence now without appearing most peculiar, so in fluent but inaccurate Italian he apologised for the trouble and asked for another pair of trousers.

'Surely your friend isn't Italian?' asked the pedrone of us.

'No, he's French, but, anyway, he's one of us,' snapped Giuliano, and we left it at that.

### *Ninth Day*

SOON after dawn next morning we tumbled out of our straw bed, sneezed the last lurking odours of the bogus Frenchman out of our lungs, inhaled the crisp mountain air, washed in the cold mountain spring, and were ready for the next day's pilgrimage. By now the convoy had taken on a more or less standard formation: Giuliano in front, waltzing away to the skyline, Renzo attending faithfully on me, Frank a little further behind, and finally Alfredo, padding along like an aged spaniel, in boots twice too big for him. We talked little. My mind was mostly a blank, scarcely noticing even the swirling chestnutted hills, the tiny clearings profuse with terraced vines, the stony mule-track on which we walked. Thus we became numb to the vastness of the journey ahead of us.

Towards noon we climbed into a rather large village, the commune of this particular area. Resting on the parapet in front of the church, we were able to read the Fascist and German posters on the wall of the village hall opposite. The requisition of arms, the call-up of all Italians of military age, the 'amasso' of farm products, the announcement of an award—the equivalent of twenty English pounds—plus extra rations of food and tobacco, to any who handed over an English or American POW. 'They,' the notice said, 'are ravaging your countryside, entering and destroying your homes, insulting your women. It is your duty to deliver these brigands—set loose by the treachery of Badoglio—to the German authorities. If you don't, you will suffer the death penalty.'

Whether it was this interesting notice, or the embarrassing episode of the cesspit, or perhaps merely one of those quick Italian decisions for no special reason, I shall not know. But Renzo suddenly came up and said they were going to leave us here, as they had decided to make for the coast and catch a train. It was quite a sentimental parting, there in the village square, overshadowed by unfriendly notices, watched by the black-coated peasants, who might be friends and might be foes, but whom we prayed would think we were all Italians. We swapped addresses, Renzo gave me two pairs of socks and a razor and some needles and thread from the cheap attaché case he had carried all this way. Alfredo gave us his last piece of Red Cross soap. We shook hands with many expressions of 'Auguri' and 'Buona Fortuna' and 'Tante belle Cose'. Then they moved down the muddy path towards the coast, while we turned southwards up the hill again. We waved, and then the corner of the school hid us from view.

After a momentary feeling of aloneness, Frank and I were glad to be rid of our Italian companions. Their method of progression—sudden bursts of walking punctuated by many long halts, and talks with everyone we met—was aggravating. And they were prepared to take risks—like entering large villages—which were too great for us. Our pilgrimage now would be much more economical in energy, more direct, and safer.

Our track climbed to a saddle, from which we looked down over a wide valley to wooded hills beyond. Up here there was a single house, dominating the landscape, and we decided its owners should give us lunch.

My introductory remarks, describing us as Italian soldiers from France, were met with polite reserve. As things seemed to be going stickily, I threw caution to the winds and admitted we were English. Immediately the padrone's attitude changed. 'Your friend is so blond I thought he might be German,' he explained, leading us up the outside staircase to the parlour and introducing us to his wife, two children, and a vast minestrone, already on the table.

'Yes,' he said, as we helped ourselves for the second time, 'these Germans are terrible. Mascalzoni! Briganti! They take everything: grain, animals, wine. They have confiscated everything mechanical, even sewing machines. I have had to hand in my shotgun, and can no longer shoot for the pot.'

'But I heard you shooting as we came up the hill.'

'Well, yes, I have a second gun, which they will never get off me... Are you real English or American? I like the English. I used to be in South America—working on the railway, you know—and met many Englishmen. We are waiting for you to deliver us from these ruffians. Why do you come so slowly? How long do you think it will be?'

'It will all be over before Christmas, for certain. But it is difficult country, you know. Our tanks can't operate very easily.'

'Then why don't you land at Genoa, or Spezia? The Germans talk of "protecting" us from the Anglo-Americans, but we don't want to be protected by those swine. We want the British to come; we know you'll look after us after the war.'

(Renzo's opinion of this sort of conversation used to be 'Protectors! Liberators! Why can't they all leave us alone?')

This was the first of many mealtime conversations with Italian country people and quite typical. The universal belief was: 'England will pull our chestnuts out of the fire.' There was no sense of shame or of defeat. On the contrary, as a nation, they had been devilishly clever in joining the winning side. It was all the fault of the Fascists that they had been dragged into this 'pasticcio'. They loathed Mussolini and Ciano with an intense flame. They feared the Germans. They considered it England's duty to put them on their feet again. One of them even said to me once: 'It is America's fault we are in this mess. She should never have allowed Germany to get so strong.'

But never, never, was it Italy's fault that she was suffering so much. The phrase 'A country gets the Government it deserves' would just not be understood by the mass of Italians.

After lunch the padrone saddled his mule and we went down together to a village, at which, he said, we might get shoes repaired. He whispered to the cobbler that we were English, and told him not to say a word about it, but as usual the news was round the village in no time. Once again the cobbler's verdict was that the shoes were beyond repair. However, we went upstairs and had a good shave and a wash, so the visit was not entirely wasted. When we came down, the shop was full of spectators come to take a stare at the foreigners, so that we sneaked hurriedly out and down the road feeling most uncomfortable, as if the eyes of the Führer himself were upon us.

That evening found us in a 'village green' landscape. Rich grass, isolated farms, fat flocks of geese and ducks … and Germans. Our search for a lodging was spoilt by a local peasant who attached himself to us and whom we thought it better to keep in ignorance of our nationality. So that we didn't like to branch aside and ask for lodging in a private house, when he had already pointed out an inn to us in a small village on the saddle of the mountain. We couldn't tell him that for us inns and villages were taboo.

So we marched on, late into the evening, until our unwanted companion finally left us. Then we tried one farmhouse. The padrone said that as he was the local podestà (mayor) he couldn't shelter English people, but there was always the inn up there... There was nothing else for it. We climbed to the village of Casone—five houses and a pub. Casone stood on a col between two peaks, a link between two different worlds. On this side were the geese and the farms and the rich light and shade cast by a setting sun in cumulus. On the other side was a steep-sided valley, heavily wooded, uninhabited, wreathed in mist, and in the perpetual gloom of an impending thunderstorm.

In the red-and-white Osteria were half a dozen ruffians talking an unintelligible dialect, and the barmaid. There was a sudden silence when we entered and sullen eyes glowered at us. Could she please tell us where to stay the night? It wasn't possible to stay in Casone. Could we have some food? No, there wasn't any. Could we have some wine then? A half-litre was silently produced. I tried to break the spell by saying we were English: it only increased their suspicion. Then, to add to the bizarreness, a drunk creature came in and started to behave like Caliban, very noisily.

'I think you had better go,' said the girl. 'There are some Germans about here collecting arms.'

We looked round the room and saw a pile of shotguns on a chair, and the horror of our position suddenly dawned on us. We hurried out of sinister Casone and down, down to the mist-wreathed abyss. And to complete the episode the thunderstorm burst above us with a boom like the last trump, and the rain-soaked night enveloped us.

For half an hour we walked down the track among the pine trees, until at last we made out the shadow of a small house, or rather hovel. As this seemed to be the only sign of humanity in this benighted valley, we decided to ask for shelter for the night.

Inside the small low room were four women and an old man. They received us gravely, but hospitably, and almost with awe at seeing the first two Englishmen they had ever encountered in their lives. A piece of cheese was produced and some bread (with the help of the family who lived in the other half of the hovel), and while we ate the cross-examination began. Did we come from Cairo? Well, yes, we had been to Cairo, but we lived in England. But surely Cairo was in England? No, Cairo was in Egypt. But wasn't Egypt a part of England? No, Egypt was in the Mediterranean, and England was away up to the north. At this all eyes—except those of grandfather who was deaf—opened wide in astonishment, and they leant a little closer to hear more from the strange pair of foreigners.

Was it possible for the Americans to understand the English? Yes. (I sometimes wonder whether this was the right answer.) When were we coming to liberate them? Why did we take so long?

This was the most ignorant Italian family we met in the whole of our journey, but many of their conceptions were widely held by the peasantry. How easy, then, to mislead such material by propaganda. They understood one life only—working the land, rearing a family. Birth, work, and death, under the divine guidance of God and the Virgin Mary. All things more complicated than this left them utterly bewildered Their attitude to us was typical of that overflowing quality of Italian tenderness. We were human beings in distress. Therefore we were objects of pity deserving help. I believe if we had been Germans the reception—with this family only—would have been the same. Pity is the Italians' greatest characteristic, especially self-pity. There is not a farmhouse in Italy now that does not echo to pathetic high-pitched whine of a woman: 'Povera Italia!'

We were profoundly grateful to this family; warmth and a meal; shelter from the storm; safety from danger; and finally sleep in the warm dry hay, and dreams of Germans and Calibans with twelve-bore shotguns.

### *Tenth Day*

NEXT day we moved on down the side of this long, winding valley. A pallid sun made an effort to appear, but soon gave it up, and the rain set in again. By noon we were down to the wide plain, where the Pontremoli road ran through water meadows and vegetable gardens, down to the sea. We wandered through orchards, gorging ourselves on the fat grapes and apples, searching the allotments for those small pear-shaped tomatoes, which are delicious. Then across the shallow river, under the railway, by a small bridge, gingerly across the main road, and up into the hills again on the far side. Our local intelligence told us that along this route were many Germans—in fact, that this was one of the main German prepared lines defending the body of Italy at the shoulders. Up on a spur of the hill we came to an isolated house and decided to ask for lunch, once more not saying we were English. Our reception was cold, and we had to put special passion into the hard-luck story to get any response out of them at all. Eventually the woman's heart melted: she grudgingly told us to go inside while she made us some polenta.

It was a bizarre lunch. We sat on the edge of a bench, Frank with his hat over his eyes, not saying a word: I, trying to spin a plausible yarn to two very suspicious yokels. To make matters worse, a deaf mute came in and started yammering at us. We bolted the polenta and left as quickly as we could. Later, it struck me that these people, too, probably thought we were Germans—or else they were scared stiff of helping anyone with Germans close by.

Thereafter our way led into another gloomy valley, where the chestnut trees came down to a stony torrent, and the road was at times a tunnel through the thick foliage. Here we ran into two obvious pilgrims, sheltering from the rain. As a matter of form we greeted them in Italian, but our disguise must have been more obvious than theirs, for their reply was in English. They were an officer and a sergeant from a prison camp near Parma. The day after the armistice, their entire camp had marched out by platoons into the nearby woods, wished on their way by a friendly commandant. Two hours later German troops arrived to take over the camp. The commandant alone was there to meet them, like a brave sea captain sticking to his doomed ship. The ex-prisoners stayed in the woods several days, fed and clothed by the locals, then split into smaller numbers and went their own ways.

Four, we thought, was too much of a crowd, so we went on and they gave us fifteen minutes start. This valley seemed interminable, getting narrower and more twisty. Occasionally the road passed through a village, where it became a quagmire, and we became objects of curiosity, walking in so much rain. We had just emerged from one of these villages, crossed the torrent by a bridge, and were climbing the stony track into the chestnuts again, when we were hailed from the window of the mill and invited in. Oh hell, we thought, here we are at five o'clock in the evening, utterly miserable, with not much prospect of finding an isolated house farther on. Let's take a risk. So we turned back and accepted.

Of course, they had recognised us for Englishmen, and, thank God, they were Anglophiles of the most valid type. The miller was fat and jolly, his hair and eyebrows dusted with the flour, and flour in the jovial wrinkles which seamed his face. He'd been in America—Kentucky I think—years ago, wonderful years of good living and lots of money. His son was there now, serving in the American Army. America was the place, you had a good time there, but the wife—like most Italian women—yearned for her hovel on an Italian mountainside, where the neighbours talked her own language, and grubby babies crawled around in swarms, and the homely filth was inches deep. So they had come home, just before the war. We heard the story in detail in broken American, of which he was very proud, lubricated by flask after flask of wine. We sat in front of a roaring fire, drying our clothes, while his wife washed our shirts and socks. The miller chuckled and guffawed, pressed us to more wine, promised to give me a pair of boots, and told us all about his boy in America. The drunker he got, the shorter got the story, but the more often he repeated himself, until the thing became a monologue, something like this: 'My boy, oh, my boy! Good boy, that! Yes, good boy. My boy …' He threw caution to the winds: told us, to our discomfort, that the Germans had been there that morning to see how much flour he was making. But we needn't worry about Germans, they were good fellows, they had reopened his mill after it had been closed by the Fascists for three years, because it worked in competition with another, run by a member of the party. Good fellows, Germans. So were the English and the Americans, good boys. Oh, my boy...

After supper, he suddenly invited us to hear the English radio, which we readily accepted, as we were keen to know how much the army had done to shorten the distance between us.

So we paddled down the street in the inky dark, and into a neighbour's house, where a solemn crowd were already gathered round the radio, listening to Radio London in Italian.

And finally, we went back to the mill again, where he put us to bed in a double bed, in a tiny room, almost over the big wheel. The air was rich with the smell of flour, and appallingly damp. But this was our first bed for a week, and we revelled in it.

### Eleventh Day

WE WERE called early in the morning by a much-changed miller. His dreams had been of Germans, and he had awakened to the full horror of his embarrassing situation: helping escaped prisoners—'la pena di morte'. We were given a quick breakfast and hustled out of the house. Worst of all, he said he could not possibly give me his boots: they were all he had. Mercifully the rain had gone: we walked under a picture-poster blue sky, over wooded hills, and down valleys, where little tributaries meandered and conjoined and weaved their way to the sea.

In one of these valleys we came to a sizeable village—the sort of village which looked as if it would have a cobbler's shop. We found it in the main street, as usual the meeting-place for the village idlers. Here we were recognised immediately by one of the idlers, who had met Frank about a week before. Then, he had been a fugitive soldier walking home like us. Now, he was home, living on his capital, keeping a weather-eye open for Germans, waiting for the British to come. As usual, too, it was almost impossible to talk business, which was the buying of shoes. The loungers wanted to hear our story. They brought us wine, treated us as equals—just deserting soldiers.

'But I want a new pair of boots,' I said, showing my sacking-covered feet, and, by a miracle, the cobbler produced from under his bench, like a conjuror with his rabbit, a brand new pair of canvas boots, exactly my size. Three hundred and fifty lire (five pounds). The deal was clinched in no time. I had his flimsy boots, canvas uppers, and compressed cardboard soles with leather bars, like football boots. He took my forlorn shoes, which, in the fine black leather of the uppers, still showed signs of their aristocratic birth. My new ones were called 'scarpe di riposo'—rest boots, a shatteringly inappropriate name.

We went on. Up more wooded hills, down more deep valleys. Fivizzano appeared—dreaded German-infested town of white houses and red roofs, big hotels filled no doubt with storm troopers, the usual spider's web of electric pylons and cables, and the broad main road, winding round the hillside, southwestwards to Spezia. We crossed this road where it crossed a gorge, by a concrete suspension bridge, and terrified ourselves by our own temerity. It might have been guarded, we told ourselves afterwards, and vowed once more never to take such risks. We were pretty German-minded by this time, probably the effect of continual stories heard from the Italians. In actual fact we had seen not one, except for their transport on the roads, and we had not approached any road until it was free from transport. But once across the Fivizzano road we could breathe freely. There were no more roads for some distance. We climbed again into the hills: rested under a big oak tree, fooled a peasant and a donkey into thinking we were Italians, and eventually reached a ridge from which we got an altogether different view. Away to the south reared the fantastic range of Carrara mountains, cutting into the sky-line like shark's teeth; at last we felt we were getting somewhere. This was on our map. We had turned the corner of the Gulf of Genoa. Emilia was almost behind us, and friendly Tuscany was close ahead.

As night approached, we found ourselves in a country of villages, but no isolated houses. We thought we would appease providence, and sleep in a cow byre instead of risking the dangers of civilisation. We found one, rather bare of leaves, but moderately clean with a spring close by, and some overburdened pear trees to rob. But while we were eating our supper on the front porch, a flock of sheep walked in the back door and took possession. So we moved on down the valley, through terraced orchards and kitchen gardens, looking for a suitable shack. Here, in the dusk, we came upon an aged couple, putting their pigs to bed. We talked to them in Italian for a while, and then, judging them friendly, admitted we were English and asked for shelter for the night. They were delighted. The old man had spent twenty years in Australia, his sons were there now. He couldn't remember much English, but promised to take us to his home and introduce us to a real hundred per cent American-speaking Wop. We waited until it was quite dark, then he led us down to the village, and to his house.

The parlour was full, as usual, of old women, old men, and babies. They were in the middle of supper, and there was enough for us—a greasy dish of fried potatoes and tomatoes. Our first grease for days. Exquisite. After supper the American was called in. He was a cut above these peasants, dressed in riding breeches, and a tweed coat—perhaps the local squire. And his accent was pure New York. He was embarrassingly pro-British (or perhaps it was just good manners). The conversation became a eulogy of the Anglo-Saxon races, and a diatribe against the Germans, with many repetitions of 'God-damn son of a bitch!' His enthusiasm was such that he told us a lot of optimistic war news, which he said he had heard himself on the English radio, but which later proved to be quite untrue. This is a very common Italian trait. Their power of self-deception is infinite. That man's enthusiasm made him genuinely believe himself that his news was true, and then he told it to us quite sincerely.

We eventually dragged ourselves away from the son of a bitch, and the old man took us out of the village and down to his hay barn, where we went to bed on the first floor, warmed by the breath of his mules, who lived on the floor below.

## *Twelfth Day*

AT DAWN a girl appeared at the barn door with a tray of milk and ersatz coffee, bread and cheese. We ate our breakfast in 'bed' while she stood watching us with friendly, wondering eyes. She was blonde and blue-eyed, and much too pretty for a peasant's daughter. We combed the straw out of our hair, put on our boots, and said goodbye to her. She smiled at us with a quiet sympathy which revealed the understanding these simple people have for fellow human beings in distress.

Frank was in one of his luxury moods. His pixie imagination was always designing the most exquisite meals, or the spacious comfort of an Italian palazzo, whose pro-British owners kept us in secret splendour as long as we wished it, then passed us safely on to their equally aristocratic relations further south. Today he wanted a monastery, the quiet peace of a cloister, the ethereal detachment from the cares and dangers of the world, and comfortable security in Abraham's bosom. And lo, we had only gone a few miles when one appeared—a sort of convent, tucked in a fold of the valley, with the traditional fish-pond, and a riotous garden which yet showed signs of many years' care and love. But we resisted the temptation to waste such a lovely day, and turned our faces again to the craggy outline of the Carrara mountains.

So we followed the contour line round the edge of the hills, through shady chestnut woods and small villages, until the hill ended, and we had to descend into the valley. Here we met a disreputable old man going home in the evening. We said we were 'militan'—he asked us to stay at his house. We followed him down the stony track, talking cautiously in Italian. I ventured to suggest that his house seemed to be too near civilisation for our safety. 'Nonsense,' he said, 'there's nothing to fear.' But the houses got more frequent, and the road more popular until we couldn't stand it any longer. 'It's unsafe for us down there,' I said, 'because we are English.'

The old man stopped, sat down on the stone wall flanking the road, and blinked. After two minutes' embarrassing silence he said: 'So you're English! Well, I sold ice-cream in Glasgow fifty years ago.' Then he jumped up and said: 'Come on down to my house,' and we were no better off than we had been before.

We reached the main road that runs south to Castelnuovo Garfagnagna, and here was a roadside pub. 'Come on, let's have a drink,' said Mr Biagioni, and before we could protest he had pushed us through the string-bead curtain into the saloon bar.

The scene resembled any English pub. All the old gaffers of the neighbourhood sitting on benches, smoking their pipes, with their glasses of wine (not the good English beer) in their hands. Behind the counter was a black-eyed Jezebel of about twenty-two.

'Bring us some wine,' piped Biagioni; 'these gentlemen are English officers.'

There was a stir of excitement among the gaffers, and the Jezebel said in perfect Cockney:

'Go on, you don't say. Hi! George, come and look at a couple of Englishmen!' So in came brother George, sleek and smart, with horn-rimmed spectacles. Both of them had spent twenty years of their young lives in East Ham; London was home to them.

We moved on, carefully side-stepping the Marcociallo of Carabinieri, out on an evening prowl, straight down the main road to Castelnuovo. By now Frank and I were practically panic-stricken, yet knew not how to extricate ourselves.

In a few minutes a voice from behind said:

'Hullo, you're Englishmen, aren't you?' The situation had become ludicrous. This was pure *Alice in Wonderland*. We looked round gingerly, expecting to see the Mad Hatter, and there was a bald middle-aged man in plus-fours, with a rucksack, and an extremely pretty wife.

Quickly he introduced himself as Mr Webb, of the Shell Company, interned on the outbreak of war, released at the armistice, now living with his Italian wife and child in Castelnuovo—waiting for something to happen. He suggested we go home with him, but we didn't fancy walking right into the town, and we hated to appear rude to our ice-cream man. Nor, for that matter, did we really believe Mr Webb. It was much more likely that he was a German. We were thoroughly uncomfortable.

Just then a lorry passed, a red civilian vehicle, with half a dozen kids in the back. The ice-cream man held up his hand and it stopped. 'Come on,' he said, 'let's take a lift.' So we jumped on the back and rumbled off down the hill, leaving the Webbs behind.

Ten minutes later he stopped it outside a great shabby house, just at the edge of the built-up area. This was the. Biagioni home and tailor shop.

Inside, we were met by Mrs Biagioni, a typical old Italian country woman, and their lovely elegant daughter. The wife hardly shared her husband's enthusiasm over us—she saw the risky side of it—but the daughter took us in charge, equipped us with towels and soap, and led us to the washplace in the garden. Here we shaved, in a sort of horse trough, surrounded by chickens and pigs.

Biagioni took us upstairs to the parlour. Here, in a room decorated with hideous virgins and ornate candelabra, was a table covered with a clean cloth, three sets of implements each, cut glass, and decanters of red wine. We sat down—the three of us men only. Mother stayed in the kitchen to cook, daughter served us. Mushroom soup, pasta, veal cutlets and poached eggs, fruit and custard—red wine—cigars. The incongruousness of it all was bewildering—the clash between the elemental peasant and the Glasgow ice-cream man. The peasant mother, the disreputable old tailor and the produce of their love and labour—their refined, well-educated, self-assured, smart daughter. This is the returned Italian emigrant, who comes back to his modest surroundings with his pockets bulging with dollars, not to be used for his own pleasure, but for educating his offspring up to a standard far above his own. From Whitechapel to West End in one generation.

To crown this fantastic day, we were shown to bed in a huge double feather bed, in a comfortable room, where we slept like logs, and wondered if we should wake up to reality.

### Thirteenth Day

DURING our brief talk yesterday with Mr Webb he had tried to dissuade us from our hare-brained project of walking to the British lines, and to go instead to a small village up in the hills, where he assured us we should be among friends, secure from the attentions of interfering Germans. He himself had just taken a house up there, where he proposed to install his wife and child and wait for the arrival of the conquering army. In principle, we thoroughly disagreed with his passive ideas, but I had for some days been suffering from a boil on the hip, and now my groin was swelling, so that a few days' rest seemed advisable.

Webb called for us at six-thirty in the morning. We had half expected that he would turn up with an armed escort to carry us off to another prison, himself now dressed in his true colours— the uniform of the Gestapo. But no, he was alone, bare-headed and bald, in good English tweeds and with a monstrous rucksack on his back, bulging with food and the necessary utensils for us to set up home. Our astonishing luck was in once more.

We walked back up the main road to Roggio, then turned up a track which followed a valley into the heart of the hills, running beside a cascading stream, past ancient mills and vine-covered farm houses. After a mile or two the path turned away up the hillside, and wandered among the deep green chestnuts, crossed gullies by stepping stones or flimsy wooden bridges, past stone 'matatas', smoking from every pore, where the chestnut flower is dried, and the fire never goes out for three months. Up, up into the chestnut jungle, until the green curtain suddenly paled, and the rain-soaked sky appeared through the tree trunks. This, said Mr Webb, was Roggio.

Frank and I halted, while Webb went on to locate his landlord, Mr Abrami, who, he hoped, would be able to direct us to a shepherd's hut, where we could live without the whole village knowing we were there.

In twenty minutes they returned. Mr Abrami shook hands and spoke to us in perfect Cockney. Twenty years of his life he had spent in East Ham. The smoke and squalor and noise of the big city were his home—not this lovely, untouched wilderness in the Tuscan hills.

There was a hut on the far side of the village, which would probably suit us. Frank and I were to walk round the village and rejoin the other two, who would go through, calling at their house on the way. We set off on our detour and soon emerged from the wood into a small cultivated valley. There were small grass fields, and hoary almond trees, and apple orchards, and vegetable gardens. Beyond, the hillside rose again to a wilderness of scrub, where sheep grazed. It had the tidy appearance of some remote Swiss Alp.

We ran into trouble almost immediately. We were spotted by about twenty young men, obviously deserters from the army, who were hoeing a field. We failed to convince them that we were Italians from Bolzano, and when it was obvious that we were being taken for Germans we eased the situation by admitting we were English. The whole of Roggio, of course, would know it within an hour.

Upon the far hillside, above Roggio, we waited for Webb and Abrami. And here we made the acquaintance of a shepherd woman. She was old, grey-haired, but her body had the strength and shape of a man's, and her bright blue eyes flashed with a strange fire. She talked loudly, throwing out her hands in an all-embracing gesture. Her words, her laugh, her suppressed excitement, expressed a joy of living which was almost frightening. While we talked, there was a droning in the air, and a hundred and twenty-eight Fortresses, in close formation, rumbled their untroubled way across the sky towards Bologna. 'British!' cried the shepherdess. 'Every day they come to bomb the Germans. The British and Americans will land at Spezia, you will see, and drive these miserable Germans out of our country.' Soon there was the dull boom of distant bombs, and then the hundred and twenty-eight rumbled back towards the sea, as steady as rocks, as disciplined as the guards.

We had obviously missed Webb, so Frank went off to look for him, while I, who found walking difficult by now, sat down with the shepherdess. After two hours, a boy came down the hill saying he had seen them up at the top, so I walked on, and arrived there at the same time as Frank, who had found them by a different route.

Mr Abrami left us, and Webb, Frank and I sat down among the leaves in the empty shepherd's hut to eat our lunch of meat pie, cake and fruit, while a rain-squall raged outside.

Suddenly there was a thump on the roof, a thump on the ground outside our countersunk hut, and a voice said: 'Cor bloody mighty—Englishmen.' And there was a tall, lanky youth of about eighteen, peering into the hut, like Khan into Mowgli's cave.

Then the words came tumbling out of his mouth, jostling each other in their urgency. Perfect Cockney.

'I'm a boy scout, and anything I can do to help I want to help. If yer don't believe me, look at me belt. Once a boy scout, always a boy scout. My home's in London. I don't want to live in this bloody country. I want to go to London....'

Bruno Peretti had certainly introduced himself. Then we heard a woman's voice outside. Bruno went out, and soon a chorus of the foulest language jangled in our ears.

'What the bloody hell are you doing here? I told you not to come. You're always in the bloody way; get to hell out of it.'

'But I had to come, Bruno, I just had to see them. English! The first English I've seen for three years.'

She was framed in the doorway. A thin, pathetic figure, dripping rain from her wispy hair. Her extraordinarily long, thin fingers twisted and untwisted. She reminded me of Mrs Bindle. This was Mrs Peretti, Bruno's mother, English bred and born. Once a poor Cockney girl, infatuated by the hot charm of an Italian restaurateur. Married to him. Thrown out of England in 1939 because he was a rabid Fascist (and now the only one in Roggio). Dumped for the duration in a primitive mountain village, where life consisted of finding, preparing, and eating such food as nature was prepared to offer—chestnut flour, walnut flour, fruit, tomatoes, a little maize. Now and again an egg or two, but not very often. A thousand miles from the cosy squalor of north London, from cinemas, and fish and chips, and a bath to keep the coal in….

'Cor! You poor boys must have suffered! I've suffered, too—suffered terribly!' She was a pathetic sight, this uprooted piece of England, with none of the stoic resistance of the Italian woman to the hardness of life. I felt glad when Bruno, with a further flourish of bad language, drove her whimpering down the hill.

Webb then left us, and Frank and Bruno went off in the rain to look for a more suitable hut—one where there was some bedding. I stayed behind, and tried to adjust my mind to this extraordinary place, where everyone seemed to talk perfect Cockney.

Soon they returned, having found a better hut. We moved down there and settled in. On the empty ground floor we made a fire and cooked our supper—the remains of the meat pie and some eggs Webb had given us. Then we turned in on the first floor in a bed of damp clover and shivered through a miserable night.

## Fourteenth Day

THE FOURTEENTH day of liberty. The importance of the present has dimmed the past into a pale memory, and the future is equally remote. Once we were in a prison camp. One day, sometime, we shall be in England, or in another prison camp. The odds are hardly worth considering, for our fate seems controlled by a higher destiny.

This morning we moved into a shepherd's hut right on the crest of the Roggio hills, about three thousand foot level. Westward, the ground fell steeply—first the grass, then heather and sparse beech trees, then the luxurious chestnuts—to a tiny red and white village, two thousand feet below in the valley bottom. Vagli Sopra it was called.

'There are Germans there,' said Bruno. 'Impossible,' we thought. There can be nothing sinister about such a charming spot.

Behind Vagli Sopra reared a mountain mass. So fantastic it almost seemed it must be artificial. Unsupported on any side, it rose by itself from the landscape, from a base of coppery beech woods to a jumble of peaks and pinnacles, and razor edges, more like an opera backdrop than the genuine article. These were the Carrara mountains, from which comes the best marble in the world. In pre-sanction days the mountains were alive to the sound of pick and blasting. Men came from villages far away to earn good pay in the quarries. Even Roggio in those days was a mining village, though her workers had to walk for three hours over the mountains to their work, and three hours back again. But sanctions, and the high cost of the marble (due to immense transport difficulties), slowly throttled the industry, and today, in wartime, the quarries are almost as dead as the Duke's Road which winds its ridiculous way over these pinnacles to suit the whim of some mediaeval princeling, who wanted to be able to say he had driven his coach right over the top.

Our new house was a stone hut six feet high and eight feet square, its stone roof flush with the grassy hillside, a doorway

five feet high, and enough chinks in the walls to let the draught
in and the smoke out. Close by were two small capannas, roofed
and walled with straw thatch. One was the sheep pen, the other
a store of dried heather for bedding. The latter we used as our
sleeping quarters. The owner of all this was a Signor Mentessi, a
shepherd from Lucca, who came up here every year in May with
his family of ten and his flock of forty (how the latter supported
the former is a mystery) and returned to the warmer climate
of Lucca in October. In fact, he had left this very day and his
hearth was still warm when we moved in.

Our house-warming was heralded by extraordinary weather,
the sort of thing only mountains can give you. All day long it
blew a westerly gale with unceasing rain. The wind whipped in
through the cracks on one side and took the smoke neatly out the
other, so that if you could avoid the line of fire, you neither caught
cold nor coughed, and the hut was fairly comfortable. Then, at
night, fell an amazing calm. But some mischievous immortal in
the Carrara mountains seemed to have been storing the gale and
now released it at us in the form of supercharged gusts. One at a
time they came tearing down the mountain and across the valley,
thundered over our heads and clattered into infinity like monster
skittle balls rolling down the alley of the sky, leaving behind such
an absolute stillness that their increasing distance could almost
be measured by the contrast. Lying in my bracken bed, I found
myself taking quite an interest in the game. Would the Marble
God bowl a straight one this time? Here it came, full pitch, right
over the top of us, roaring like a wild bull, and away, away again
into space. Then the hush. Even the mice stopped their annoying
gambols in amazement.

It was cold in the capanna, even with three feet of bracken
on top of you. The place was just wide enough for the two of
us to lie side by side. For me, the discomfort was excruciating,
trying to avoid lying on my boils or bumping them into
Frank. The wind crept in from all sides, and up from below,

penetrating the bracken nest, our clothes, our very bones. We imagined ourselves leading this life in an Italian winter—three feet of snow on the ground and a remorseless north wind.

By now we were connoisseurs of Italian bedding. We had experimented with all the more rustic varieties: hay, straw, bracken, leaves, grass. This, I think, is the order of merit, with hay a long way first. For softness, impermeability to wind, and smell, it was unbeatable. Usually, too, it was associated with the rich warm steam of oxen, sleeping on the floor below. Straw was fairly soft, but let the wind through, and weaved itself into one's socks and pullover abominably. Bracken was too spiky—long hard stalks which inevitably pricked you in the eye, or nudged you in the tenderest places. Leaves, usually chestnut or beech, were entirely incohesive. Turn over, and they would go scuttering away, leaving you naked to the blast. And they contained an uncomfortable high percentage of prickly chestnut husks. Grass was soft and sweet-smelling, and atrociously damp.

### Fifteenth Day

DAYLIGHT came at last. An apologetic sun smiled wanly, as though ashamed of the night's orgy, but soon gave up the struggle and retired behind the grey rainsoaked clouds. We set about making our stone hut habitable.

Yesterday evening we had had a visit from a Mrs Ferrari. The dear lady had walked through the rain from Roggio, bringing a basketful of rice, potatoes, wine and milk, sugar, salt and bread, for us. So we did not go without breakfast. It is principally to Mr and Mrs Ferrari and their nephew George that we owe an unrepayable debt for caring for us during our week at Roggio. Nothing was too much trouble for them. No weather was too bad for them to make the hour's uphill walk from the village, bringing food, or news, or magazines. No risk or sacrifice was too great for them. In a sense, we were countrymen, for they had lived twenty years in London, until Cockney became their language, the smoke and bustle of Leyton their very existence. George's parents were there still running their small restaurant, surviving boycotts and insults and anti-Italianism, for the sake of their adopted home. George himself, in fact, was a British subject, for he had been born there and spent sixteen of his twenty years in England. But that was a secret, not even known to most of the Roggites.

George came to see us after breakfast, with more food, and some old—but wartime—copies of *Life*—the first English we had read in a fortnight. He is dark, and full-lipped, with a thin toothbrush moustache, which makes him look more than twenty. His worn clothes were unmistakably English—relics of his better days. He had come back to Italy just before the war, to finish his education at college at Pisa. And there they had caught him, and made him a soldier. He is intelligent and level-headed, and his unusual ability soon earned him the job of sergeant radio mechanic. They never sent him to the front, for he told them he didn't want to fight the English. Such an act of sentimental generosity could only be perpetrated by an Italian general staff!

When the armistice came he was in the barracks at Florence. The Germans were there almost at once, surrounding the place with troops, and tanks on the corners. The Italian general, like most of them, preferred prudence to heroics, and yielded without a fight. His officers and men were then given a choice— either to go as prisoners to Germany, to work in factories and farms, or to enlist in the German Forces. George was advised by a young officer that their only hope of escape lay in pretending to join the Germans. That afternoon, three hundred of them, all 'volunteers', were marched out of the town to a big wood, where they were to camp. They went in sections of threes, three files of Italians, then one of German guards, and so on. Once in the woods, George's young officer bribed the nearest German section to say nothing, and the two of them slipped out of the ranks and away. George then got some plain clothes and walked home to Roggio in three days. Others had done the same, till Roggio now housed some twenty deserters, all working on the land, with their sentries posted on the approach paths through the woods to give warning of any Germans. He promised that we, too, would be instantly told of any danger—which went a long way to reconcile us to this week of waiting.

After George had gone, Frank went off to collect firewood and water from the spring, two hundred yards down the hillside, while I prepared the lunch, and poulticed my boils in a somewhat primitive way.

Lunch consisted of boiled rice, boiled potatoes and castagnaccio—a delicious cake made (by Mrs Ferrari, not me) out of chestnut flour. Unbalanced diet, it is true, but this was our usual fare, starch and more starch … and hence boils.

As we finished our meal, there was a sudden hubbub outside, and next minute the entire Mentessi family gushed in to see us. The weather was too bad for them to start the journey to Lucca, so they had folded their flock at Roggio and come up to see how we were getting on.

Signor Mentessi was a typical Italian shepherd—the most exhilarating type of person to be met in the whole of Italy. There is something intensely vital, unrepressed, about these shepherds. They are above the squalor and misery of war. Life to them is a thing of beauty and urgency, to be savoured, every minute of it, to be indulged in without restriction. They live very close to the gods on Mount Olympus, and very close to heaven, too.

He was dressed, like most Italian shepherds, in black velvet breeches, black velvet coat, and black homberg, and carried not the traditional crook, or stick, but an umbrella. In fact, to the romantic-minded, he was definitely disappointing as a shepherd, but none the less his curious appearance was intriguing. He was followed by his family—the males in descending sizes dressed in various styles ranging from black velvet for the eldest to a disreputable cluster of rags for the youngest; and the females in the flimsiest of frocks, more suitable for a tea dance than an autumn mountainside. Around about gambolled a number of dogs, only kept in control by continual whistling.

His frank, blue eyes opened wide in astonishment as he saw our attempt at a fire. He dashed outside and soon returned with armfuls of sticks and branches, which he threw on the flames until they roared to the ceiling. Then out again to fetch a plank from the fienile, which he broke in two between two stones in the hut wall and quickly fashioned into a seat. We all crammed into the hut, the men sitting round the fire, sweat and soot running down our faces, the women standing behind, with the shadows dancing across their shiny cheeks. Bread was produced, no niggling ration, but monstrous hunks of the stuff which Mentessi sliced with a single broad stroke of his sharp knife. And we ate, though we'd eaten but a few minutes before. I must make it clear that there was nothing excitable or hysterical about all this, but rather was it an effusion of generosity and urgent desire to make the most out of life. He did my inhibitions a power of good.

### Sixteenth Day

SUCH WAS our life at Roggio for a whole week. We rose stiffly from our cold bed each morning about eight, usually to a day of rain and wind. Sometimes we were woken by the bluff voice of Mr Ferrari, out on an early poaching expedition with his dog and his twelve bore. Mr Ferrari is rather like Groucho Marx— the same stoop, the thick glasses, the long nose curving over the droopy moustaches. He was full of character and a dry sense of humour. Highly volatile and excitable, he yet feared nobody. Like most Italians, he was entirely unmoved by the German ban on arms. Even the threat of death would not make him relinquish his gun. But one morning George arrived, to say that his uncle had accidentally shot his dog (the only thing he did shoot while we were there). He had burst into tears and was quite inconsolable. His dog was dearer to him than his wife, I believe.

After breakfast Frank would usually go on a scavenging expedition, returning with firewood, potatoes, mushrooms. I would 'do the housework'—or go down the hill to our spring to wash. As my hip got better, we went for short walks round the Roggio plateau, revelling in the ever-changing view of mist and mountains, sunlight and shadow, brilliant green fields and flaming beech trees, spread out below to all points of the compass.

Each day we were visited by one of the dear housewives of Roggio, bringing us rice and bread, jam, chestnut cake, even eggs. God knows, they had little enough themselves, but they never hesitated to share what they had.

One day we had a visit from a stocky little individual in plus-fours and an old Trilby hat. He had the long leathery face and blue eyes of the mountaineer. This was another Mr Peretti, a native of Roggio but an old Alpini who had spent most of his life on the Mont Blanc massif. He offered us a new secure home in his matata down in the valley. There, at least, we should be warm, living in the smoky atmosphere of roasting chestnuts, with a fire which would not be extinguished until December. But already we were feeling restless.

And once Frank returned with another English prisoner. This was Sergeant Knowles from Chiaveri camp. There, also, the Germans had arrived immediately after the armistice. They also were taken off to entrain for Germany, but instead of taking with them their private gear, they concealed in their bundles picks, saws and knives. Once in the train, they had commenced to hack their way out, and a number had thus escaped. He had joined up with a Scotsman, who was slowly drinking his way through Italy, sponging from village to village, and inevitably destined for recapture, as Sergeant Knowles sensibly realised.

He left him while the going was good, and was now making his way south alone.

On the Thursday night we were invited down to the Abramis' house to hear the radio. This was a thing we were very keen to do, for we heard so many rumours of the position of the allied troops that it was imperative that we get some sort of truth.

George came to fetch us at dusk and we walked down in the gloaming, cautiously circled the village and entered the house secretly from the back. Here we found old Abrami and his wife and three attractive daughters sitting round a roaring fire. George, who was engaged to the youngest, got into a huddle with her in the corner. How strange it seemed to our monastic minds, this youthful courting. It seemed to stir long-buried feelings inside one, like the first flicker of spring after the long grim winter.

This was England, not Italy, this scene round the fire. The women were treated equally with the men. The men showed them courtesy. They dressed well, and were proud of their appearance. London had influenced their life more than Roggio.

Then began an orgy of radio listening: Radio Bari, Radio Algiers, Radio London, Radio Roma, Berlin in Italian, Berlin in English... From it all dawned the realisation that our troops were still very far away, and not likely to come on very quickly. There and then we decided to move on as soon as possible.

When the radio programmes finished, Mrs Abrami produced a poached supper for Frank and me, and we talked of Italy and England. The hearts of these people, springing from the earthy stock of Tuscany, lay far away in the capital of a foreign country. Their eyes glowed as they told the story of their life in Leyton, living in an almost entirely Italian community, keeping their little restaurant, travelling on the trolley bus: yes, even taking their twelve bores to the country at weekends in search of rabbits. It is a strange thing, this Italian migration. One man from a small village goes abroad to seek his fortune.

After years, he returns with his pockets bulging and tales of a far away eldorado, where everyone is happy, everyone is well fed, everyone has work. And they do work! Fourteen hours a day they work, building roads, digging in the mines, boring tunnels—all the sweated labour which a more northern race would scorn to do for such a pittance. But to them, who know only the poverty of rural Italy, it is a fortune. Then more families, fired by these rosy tales, emigrate and return eventually to their Italian homes, so that you find this village have all been to London, and that to Bristol, and that one to Ohio, or New York. Here, in Tuscany, they are mostly migrants to England. In southern Italy the majority go to America.

In their adopted land the men rapidly assume the local characteristics. They learn the language, they dress like the natives, they mingle with them and learn their habits. They lose their old patriotism, and usually wish to remain, calling themselves American or English; but the women are never assimilated. They live in their own Italian community, almost in a purdah, scarcely learning to speak the language, and their yearnings are always towards home—the poor, wretched hovel where they were born and bred. It is the women who cause these Italian families to return home—as most of the men will grumblingly tell you.

And then you get the most curious situations. Often we met a family who had sons fighting on both sides. I was even asked why it wasn't possible for a son in the American Army to make an allotment to his mother in Italy. The war of nationalities, you could see, was complete anathema to them. They had no patriotism, no national pride. Their disarmingly logical minds are not confused by ideas of loyalty or honour. They have their idea of honour, certainly, but it is quite different from ours.

There is something terrifyingly defeatist in their attitude now. Mussolini they loathe with an undying, livid fury. Ciano, perhaps, was even more hated. It was Ciano who called for a patriotic relinquishment of gold wedding rings, and then was caught with two suitcases full of them, trying to make his getaway into Switzerland. But they had no faith, either, in their royal family. Most were agreed that the King must go. They blamed him for ever allowing Mussolini to get so far—and few would hear of the accession of the king's son. In fact, to put it shortly, they had no political ideas, no faith in the future. All they wanted was to be left alone to farm their land in peace.

Somewhere after midnight we decided it was time to go home. But outside it was blowing and raining like the mouth of hell, and the prospect of an hour's walk was uninviting. Mr Ferrari offered to put us up in his fienile, and there we slept, in rustic luxury, with pillows and eiderdown to keep us from actual contact with the hay, and centrally heated by two donkeys, on the floor below.

Next morning Ferrari called us early and guided us out of the village before anyone was about. It was a miserable enough walk up to our cabin in the rain.

We spent the day clearing up, in preparation for leaving. Signor Mentessi had left the place spotless for us, so we must do the same for him. Our lunch was a huge stew of boiled rice and mushrooms. Our supper was the last remaining potatoes, baked in the ashes of our last fire.

We were both glad to be on the move. My boils had almost cleared, and I felt much better and fitter. Each of these last few days I had been getting more restless, hardly knowing how to amuse myself in the idle hours in the hut, hardly able to think of anything but the big adventure before us. Frank was much more placid and adaptable. Blessed with an active, puckish imagination, he told me one improbable story after another, as we sat over the dying embers of our fire in the evenings, listening to the rain outside and the rats chasing our food. In fact he supplied all the entertainment value and I none. I could not have found a more perfect companion.

We went for our last walk that evening, round the horseshoe top of the Roggio tableland. Away to the west the clouds were breaking on the Carrara peaks.

Steamy wreaths climbed languidly from the red roofs of Vagli Sopra, evaporating into the pale blue sky. As the sun set, a great shadow fell on the landscape, and those jagged mountains stood out starkly against the pink and yellow backcloth. Then the sky darkened and a million stars pushed their timid lights through the gloom, and there was a great peace over Tuscany. We remembered the local weather lore: when Monte Massa is clear of cloud, the weather will stay fine. Yes, the moment had come to move on.

Daily air fleets over. Many explosions from direction of Pisa, Livorno. Local expectations of a landing.

### Twentieth Day
### Saturday, 2nd October, our twentieth day of liberty.

WE WERE packed and ready to leave before dawn. A final sweep out of the hut, and we were off down to Ferrari's for breakfast. Here we collected our clean clothes, which the dear lady had washed. George insisted on our taking a spare pair of trousers each, a pullover, a blanket and spare shirts. We stuffed ourselves with poached eggs and bacon, bread and butter and jam and coffee, while the Ferrari family jumped around in an excess of hospitality, and the three Abrami girls came in and looked suitably sympathetic and charming. They were obviously all captivated by the romance of this odyssey. George himself was torn between a desire to come with us or to stay with his sweetheart. The sweetheart was the more certain of the two alternatives, and although we should quite have liked him with us as guide and interpreter, we never really thought he would come.

We made our profuse goodbyes at last and set off down into the chestnut woods with George and poor lame Bruno accompanying us part of the way. Then they, too, turned back, and we were alone again, with three-hundred miles of mountains between us and our armies. I think really the Roggites, who, though hospitable, were a timid crowd on the whole, were glad to see us go. And we felt infinitely content to be on the road again.

It was a most perfect morning, absolutely cloudless. The Carrara range was a faint outline of darker blue in the eternal blueness of land and sky. There was gentleness and beauty in the atmosphere, and a sense of expectancy and joy, too. The sun came up and pierced our green umbrella with pools of brilliant light.

We dropped down to the valley, and along the stream to the main road. Down again, through kitchen gardens and muddy farmyards, past the slender arches of the Poggio railway viaduct, down to the bed of a wide stream, which frolicked its way to the sea in a thousand changing moods: here deep and thoughtful, there serene and gracious, now racing with happy laughter over the polished stones—fickle, but always beautiful. We paddled across in one of these rapids, just where the river turned and swept into a narrow gorge between fantastic cliffs. There was something humorous about this scenery. It was grandeur on a miniature scale—a dwarf trying to make itself look important. For the cliffs were but the edge of a sugar loaf 'poggio', the torrent was but a stream. Round the corner it seemed to despair of its attempt at importance, for suddenly the river became a gentle thing, ambling through water meadows, while away on either side distantly rose the warm green hills of the Castelnuovo valley, seeming to smile at this attempted precocity in the middle of the sophisticated Tuscan scene.

We put on our boots again and climbed to the road on the east side of the valley. This was a secondary road, going in just our direction. It was deserted, for this was the Italian dinner hour.

Everything seemed so safe that we decided to walk along it.

For an hour we walked, scarcely meeting a soul. It seemed almost too good to be true that we should make such good time with so little effort. We were descending a hill to a small bridge, which spanned a gully, when two Carabinieri flashed by on bicycles, silently, and turned off into the gates of a small power house which nestled in the gully. This made us think a bit: we decided that perhaps we were taking too much of a risk. Perhaps we ought to leave the road after crossing the bridge. Then, to our horror, just as we were crossing the bridge, a car suddenly whisked down the hill behind us, and stopped with a hoot a few yards behind our backs. We saw it contained soldiers in uniform, and we knew that only Fascist soldiers still wore uniform in this country. Were they after us? Should we run, and thereby look suspicious for certain. Or should we walk nonchalantly on, looking our most innocent Italian, and risk getting caught without a chance to escape? We attempted the second method with more than a suspicion of the first in it, in our urgency to clear the bridge and reach the safety of the woods beyond. Mercifully, the occupants of the car shouted to the two Carabinieri, and then walked up to meet them. This might mean even more trouble, but at least it gave us a start. We reached the trees, sauntered guiltily off into them, and then ran like hell up the hill, across a field and into the undergrowth again. We scarcely paused until we had put about three ridges and gullies between us and that sinister bridge. At last we reckoned we had eluded any chase, and sat down to eat our lunch of hard-boiled eggs (from Roggio) on the edge of a brook, still well concealed in the bushes. This just serves us damn well right, we said to each other ruefully; never again will we trust ourselves on the road. We did, of course, on more than one occasion, but always through necessity, and with the greatest caution and misgivings.

We were now striking diagonally south-east, across ridge and gully, ridge and gully, towards the high bald crest of the mountain range. It was hard, disheartening going, but safe, at least. Eventually we found ourselves on a well-defined mule track, which zig-zagged up a long steep hillside to the village of

Silico. This was on our route: once more we seem to have got some purpose in our walking.

Plodding up this twisty track beneath the chestnut trees, we suddenly heard a strange whistling above us. It started away up the hill, and came rushing down upon us, passing overhead with a scream and fading away into the valley below. Looking up through a gap in the canopy, we saw a load of logs, bundled precariously together and attached to a pulley on a taut wire, hurtling their way down to the valley. This was how the carbonari got their trees down from the inaccessible mountain tops to the river. It was a weird noise, and would have been quite disturbing, if heard for the first time in the dark by someone who did not know its origin. It might have been a witch, passing on her broomstick to some sinister assignation.

About three o'clock, the trees thinned, and there, standing in a clearing of vineyards and vegetable gardens, was the jumbled whitewashed village of Silico. This place, we felt, was safe enough, for no road reached it, only muletracks twisting down into the green desolate valleys.

On the edge of the village we met a man teaching a small boy to fly a kite. To him we put our usual questions: were there Germans about? Were there Fascists here? He reassured us on both points and then invited us in for a glass of wine. Over the wine he told us that there were two other Englishmen in the village, and would we like to meet them? Yes, we said.

So he led us up through the cobbled, precipitous streets, past the usual village square, the church, and the mayory, to a large house standing back from the main street in a small courtyard. Still painted over the door, ominously, was the old Fascist exhortation: 'Credere, Ubbedire, Combattere.' Inside in the hall were pictures of Mussolini and Ciano and Victor Emmanuel, and more Fascist wisecracks. My bowels began to melt again. Was this a trap? Were we just being fools again? But the whole thing seemed too obvious to be possible.

The comfortable landlady met us and took us upstairs. In that room, she said, you will find another British officer. We opened the door, and there, reclining like Cleopatra on a feather bed, was Lieby! Then our fears dissolved, our guide and hostess were forgotten and we started in comparing notes.

Since jumping from the train, Lieby had had a moderately uneventful trip, as we had. In fact he had trodden a rose-strewn path for a large part of the way. He had met a woman who had fallen in love with his blue eyes and his guttural voice and had been prepared to relax the strict Italian rules of morality. He had been supplied with money and the finest maps of the country. Then he had met another South African, Sergeant Erikson, and together they continued the great pilgrimage. Now they had found this comfortable house, and, as Lieby had not been very well for a day or two, they had decided to stay awhile and recuperate.

We voiced our misgivings about the Fascist texts and pictures. Oh, the landlady had told him, this house used to belong to the local Federale, who had run away. She and her husband decided to keep the pictures up, for, she said, should any Germans or Fascists come to the village, their suspicions as to her loyalty would immediately be allayed. I didn't altogether share this ingenuous opinion. It seemed to me that any Fascist finding such a genial atmosphere of totalitarianism would immediately want to be billeted there—and then where would we be? Anyway, Lieby and Erikson had already been here two days—time enough for the landlady to get the Fascists along, if she had been that way inclined.

We all moved into the comfortable front room, whose long windows gave on to a balcony over the sun-drenched courtyard. Here we found a small boy playing on the carpet with live American incendiary bullets. Then we saw that the mantelpiece was covered with the shabby remnants of an aeroplane crash: ammunition, a microphone mask, various battered instruments, and one identity disc bearing the name of John

S. Dignam, USAAF. The day before, it appeared, a damaged Fortress, struggling home across the mountains from a raid on Bologna, had suddenly crashed into the chestnut woods behind the village, bursting into flames, and killing the entire crew. The first Italian on the scene had dashed bravely into the fire and removed the leather flying boots of the pilot—a prize to be valued above rubies. The bodies of the crew were being buried in Silico tomorrow.

The room now began to fill up with all sorts of visitors. The village priest arrived. He was the real organiser behind this help to escaped prisoners in Silico. He was running a sort of hostel in the old dopolavoro building for fugitive British, American and Italian soldiers. This house was but one of his 'billets'. He offered to try and send a message to our families through the Vatican.

Then arrived three or four of these refugee Italian officers, who had fled their homes for fear of the Germans, and were living in the hospitable security of Silico. They brought with them a number of the smart young local girls, all aflutter with self-conscious excitement. They suggested a sing-song here tonight, for which they would bring an accordion. This sort of thing was not at all what we wanted: we began to feel most uncomfortable. Luckily this carefree atmosphere was suddenly shattered by a message which came to say that Fascist bands had been formed at Lucca and were roaming the countryside looking for escaped prisoners. Immediately, all their bold braggadoccio collapsed like a bubble. A hunted, fearful look came into their eyes, and they started wondering how they could relieve themselves of the responsibility of us. All ideas of a sing-song were at once abandoned. It was considered unsafe for us all to go to the dopolavoro for supper. In the middle of all this there was a commotion outside, English voices talking execrable Italian, and there were two English padres and a major, dressed like us, in the blatant disguise of old Italian clothes, and carrying rucksacks and sticks. But they were soon whisked away by the priest to some other corner of the village, and we never saw them again.

Frank and I, Lieby and Erikson, found ourselves alone in the house with the old woman who was to give us supper. Eventually, when we had almost despaired of it, it came—a vast bubbling bowl of minestrone, bread and cheese and fruit.

About nine o'clock, while we were digesting our supper over the kitchen fire, our good lady's husband walked in. He was in business in Lucca: caught the train back to Castelnuovo each evening, and trudged the long way up the mountain to Silico. He was a typical Fascist, the hard bony face, the sleek black hair, the smooth blue suit with overpadded shoulders. We recognised him at once for one of those cold, ruthless types whose object was to keep in well with both sides and swim with whatever current caught him. He produced a little notebook, showing the names of all the British prisoners he had helped. We recognised that of Roy Cooke, who had left Gavi three months before to go into hospital in Milan. He had been there when the RAF bombed the station and hospital in August, and this was the first news we had had that he was safe. He had been here two days before us, and had delighted our host and hostess with his intelligent conversation. I could believe it: Roy is a good actor. Our Fascist now asked us for our names, and gently reminded us that, should we reach safety, we might put in a good word about him with the Allies.

This was a thing we intended to do, anyway, with all those who had helped us, but never with more reluctance than in this case. His hospitality was entirely selfish. He would as soon turn round and cut your throat if that suited him better. We saw now the reason for the Fascist emblems.

About ten o'clock a girl arrived to take us to our bedroom in the dopolavoro. Here, on the first floor of the big, gaunt building, we slept in a double bed in a well-furnished room, under the ferocious gaze of a photograph of Victor Emmanuel.

### Twenty-first Day

A GIRL gave us breakfast in the little downstairs parlour of the dopolavoro: bread, acorn coffee and wine. Meanwhile, we studied the map of the district, which every dopolavoro contains. We decided that this exasperating business of traversing the side of the range, dipping into every ravine, climbing again to every ridge, was uneconomical, and that it would be better to go out of our way for an hour or two in order to reach the crest where the going would be good. Now, also, we made one of the biggest decisions of the trip. Formerly we had intended to travel down the west coast, across the Arno, towards Rome. It was, after all, the shortest, easiest route to our lines. But now it seemed to us that the Arno presented a considerable obstacle, especially if there were Fascist bands on the look-out for fugitives on this route. We had, in fact, heard last night that one hundred and fifty British had been taken trying to cross the river. It was true, these rumours found a fertile breeding ground in the excitable minds of the Italians, but we should never forgive ourselves if we got captured through our own carelessness. We decided, therefore, to keep always to the Apennines. This meant travelling almost due east from Silico, passing north and east of Florence. The route would be much longer, but what was an extra week or two when you had been a prisoner three years?

We set off up the wooded shoulder then, accompanied by the girl's old father, who was going down into the next valley to take part in the local saint's day feast. We parted two hours later, with many expressions of good luck. Frank and I rested a moment in the gay morning sunlight, watching the old man trudging down the mule track towards a distant white village almost hidden in the thick chestnut woods. Then we turned up our own track, north-eastwards up the shoulder towards the distant blue ridge.

It was a wonderful morning: not a cloud marred the infinite blueness of this Tuscan sky. A fresh cold north-east wind swept down the ridge, vitalising every nerve and invigorating us to the point of exuberance. Life seemed very good and wonderful and mysterious. Behind us stretched the intense green valley of Castelnuovo, with beyond it the Roggio hills, and away, away in the distance, like a thread of gossamer on the blue horizon, the outline of the Carrara mountains. To the south, the hills fell away, and we could just see the plain of the Arno, and Lucca, whose historic name had acquired a new sinister ring in our minds. To right and to left of us the chestnut woods stretched to infinity, undulating like huge waves, whose troughs were the long deep valleys, which marked the paths of many streams from the source near the main range to their destination in the Castelnuovo river. Off to the left, on the next wave but one, was the main road from Castelnuovo to Madena, writhing its way up the hill to an old monastery, then dipping down again into unknown, foreign Emilia.

The mule track led us through one or two tiny villages of log huts—the homes of the carbonari—where the chickens and pigs rooted around among the huge piles of felled trees, and placid mules waited patiently to be loaded with faggots for the journey down to other villages. As we got higher, the chestnuts gave way to coppices of beach and ash, set on a carpet of that rich velvet green grass which always reminds me of Switzerland. Then the trees finished, and here were only thickets of hazel bushes, planted to break the force of the fierce north wind and prevent erosion.

Towards noon we reached the top, and looked into the eye of that tearing wind on to a panorama of jumbled mountains, range on range, with perhaps in the distance a suspicion of the great plain of Bologna, the Po valley. Now we turned southeast, along the grass ridge, which fell steeply on either side, but rose in an even gentle slope towards the distant Alpe della Tre Potenze—the Three Powers, Emilia, Tuscany, Marche, which met at this point.

A ridge walk always signified for me a period of sublime happiness. It infected me with a strange, excited feeling of ecstasy, of complete and sudden emancipation from all cares and troubles and dangers and doubts. Here the continual but almost unconscious tension in which I perpetually held myself in the valley was dissipated. Down there, there was always a possibility of danger round every corner—a German or a Fascist or a Carabinieri. One had to be constantly ready to react quickly to any emergency. But here there was no danger. We could talk and sing to our heart's content. The wind and the sun were our companions, the infinite space was our protection. These were indeed our Delectable Mountains.

The ridge soon became a razor edge, with high cliffs to the east, and to the west a steep stoney slope. Here, where the goat track wound among massive boulders and scree, crossed by many streamlets, we heard the music of sheep bells, and came upon an old man and his wife tending their flock. We decided to eat our lunch with them. They were Protestants, members of that small, much persecuted sect of Valdeans. They came from a village by Lucca, but now in the summer and autumn they brought their flock to the Alpe della Tre Potenze, living in a log cabin just below the tree line. He was old, perhaps seventy, yet his blue eyes shone with life, and his frank gaze gave the appearance of utter serenity, the perfect composure of one whose mind is untroubled by wars or politics or patriotisms or jealousies, or any complicated thought. His life was spent on the high ridge in simple contact with nature and very close to his God.

They gave us some delicious sweet chestnut polenta and some sour cheese. With difficulty we persuaded them to take some of our bread. We had also some boiled eggs from Roggio, so this was an unusually good meal. We talked of Italy, and sheep, and religion and England—anything but the war. The old wife confessed to having been in Glasgow years before, but like many Italian women abroad, she hadn't learnt the language. Meanwhile the flock of sheep and goats strayed over the ridge, and even their bells were silent.

We moved on at last, the shepherd insisting on coming with us for a mile or two, to show us the road, before climbing again to the ridge to search for his flock. We watched him scramble up the scree, turn to wave, then scramble on. Then we dipped into a sheltered fold of the hill, and stopped again for half an hour's sleep in the sun.

The track wound round again to the ridge, where it dipped down between two peaks. Ahead was the Tre Potenze, with a magnificent rock wall on the left side dropping several hundred feet to a small green basin, which spilled over again into another deep, wooded valley. Our way, well marked now by the painted signs of the climbing club, led down into this basin, and thence to the famous dago Santa, the Holy Lake. But we were destined not to see this beauty spot; it was guarded by a barbed-wire fence which, I gather, is used to indicate the forest reserve which may not be destroyed. The path sheared off to the left following a tiny stream which gathered strength as it went, twisting down the hill between the boulders, tumbling over small precipices, with a precocious roar, down, down to join the main river in the distant valley.

We were on a new stage now. This was Emilia again. Gone were the profuse chestnut woods, the terraced vineyards and cultured beauty of the Castelnuovo valley. Here the scene was more rugged: pine and oak mixed in a wilderness of undergrowth; above us the blue cliffs of the Potenze; beyond, across the valley, rose high gaunt grassy hills—the barren south-west face of the next range.

Along the valley bottom were vivid green pastures, cropped by lazy cows. Isolated farmhouses, slate-roofed, with their sides protected with a blue tin sheeting, studded the countryside.

We reached the first habitation about three-thirty. On the outskirts of a cluster of three or four farms we met an old man and two small children rounding up their cows. We stopped to ask them about the German content of this new valley. Sure enough, the old boy talked English, though I forget to which particular part of England he had been. We sat down with him in the sun, on the rich green grass, while the children continued the cow chase with much shooing and beating of sticks. He invited us to stay the night, and although the day was yet young, and we had come but a short distance today, we eventually agreed. When the cows had been caught, we all walked back to the farm, where the old man's wife appeared genuinely pleased to see us, and instantly produced an exquisite drink for us in the form of rich fresh milk.

We had hardly been indoors ten minutes when two other Englishmen arrived, looking glaringly foreign in huge straw hats, and big sacks on their backs. They were parachutist officers, captured in Tunisia, and came from the camp at Fontenellata, near Bologna—No. 29, I believe it was. We didn't feel particularly pleased to see them: there seemed to be no privacy in this country. We thought we had got clear of the well-worn Pilgrim's Way—yet here was another party travelling hot on our heels. It was not just the Englishman's dislike of being social on a journey; we felt that if the trail became too well worn the Germans might notice it, too. However, these two, after a glass of milk, moved on down the hill to another farm. We watched them go: superbly confident and incredibly English-looking. Were we really the same? Then began rather a long tedious evening. Our host disliked talking English and none of his family could. We had to spend six hours talking Italian and trying to understand a particularly difficult accent.

Various indefinable members of the family came and went, but the most intriguing was an old mustachioed grandmother who sat in the corner of the fireplace, saying never a word, but getting up regularly every ten minutes and going for a walk a hundred yards down the path and back. We wondered what particular organ in that old lady required such inconvenient treatment. And the most unpleasant member was a small boy, very effeminate, in black cloth plus-fours and an open-neck blue silk shirt, with a hair-net over his long oily locks. Most precocious, we thought him, until we learnt that he was sixteen and not ten, as he looked.

This family was in a particularly bad way. The Germans had been up the valley a few days before, confiscating and robbing. Worse, they had had no ration of bread, rice or flour for a fortnight. They were living entirely on polenta and a little cheese.

As the light faded, the wife started to prepare the evening meal. The fire was brought to a blaze of crackling faggots, and the huge iron pot, hanging on its chain from the chimney, was filled with water. When the water was boiling, the maize flour was poured in from a big bag, all of it at once, and then began a furious stirring. For ten minutes she stirred, using all her strength as the mixture stiffened into a paste. Then at just the right moment the big pot was unhooked, and the mixture was poured on to the dresser top, where, on cooling, it instantly set into a Yorkshire pudding-like substance. This was cut into slices with a knife, sprinkled with a little cheese, and served up still hot. Here was polenta in its starkest form.

We turned in about eleven o'clock that night—much later than our usual hour, for we had been promised the radio news in a neighbouring house, but that eventually failed us. Utterly tired from the strain of so much conversation, we tumbled into the hay above the cows, and slid immediately into dreamless slumber.

### Twenty-second Day

THE OLD man called us at dawn. We scrambled down from our fifteen-foot-high bed and assembled our dishevelled selves in the pale light which filtered through the crack in the high barn door. We always slept with all our clothes on, removing only our boots and coats, lying side by side with our coats for pillows and several feet of 'bedding' on top of us, and finally George's blanket over our heads. This meant that each morning there was a quarter of an hour's work removing the 'bedding' from pullover and socks, into which it wove its way in most diabolical fashion. This morning was particularly bad: our couch had been a stiff, wiry sort of hay, which had wormed its way right through to the skin, and now irritated abominably.

We went into breakfast. The good lady had cooked us chestnut porridge, piping hot and generating heat like neat rum, swamped in creamy milk and sweetened with sugar. This, I think, was the best breakfast we ever had on the whole trip. Then we collected our gear—the rolled blanket containing our spare clothes, and the canvas bag in which we kept odds and ends, toilet gear, and such (only this day our hosts had been unable to supply us with any lunch)—and set off down through the woods towards the river, accompanied for a short way by the old man, who was making one more trip to the village, in the hope of getting his flour and rice rations. As we left, Granny was just setting off on one of her ever-recurring trips down the path.

In a moment the sun came flooding over the hillside beyond the river, rising almost perceptibly into a pure blue sky. The high ridge looked blurred and sombre against that glare, but on our side of the valley the mountain suddenly became active, suffusing with intense blues and greens and reds as the sun crept valleywards over the rocks and trees. High up on the far ridge ran a darker pencil line, climbing up to the high pass by the Tre Potenze—a mule track now, but once a famous road, our late host had told us, for up this valley Hannibal had come, and Napoleon, too, their cumbersome baggage trains and eager soldiers struggling up to the pass, from which they would descend into the fertile plain of Tuscany. Now the road lay beyond the ridge, a new wide motor road, polished and blue, perfectly banked, bounded by black and white posts—the last word in an art the Fascists had inherited from their Roman ancestors. La Betone, they called it, after the pass over which it went. Now another invader was using it. Day and night his long convoys of lorries crept by, taking food and ammunition and troops to feed the Nazi armies two hundred and fifty miles to the south.

We crossed the thundering stream by a plank bridge, where a conduit led off to a nearby mill. Then up the other slope of the valley to a rough road which seemed to lead over the ridge and which seemed small enough to support no Germans. In fact it soon became a mule track of large well-laid flagstones, winding steeply up through the trees. The local peasants have to take it in turns to mend sections of these tracks, which vary greatly in quality according to the industry of the road-mender of the moment.

We came out on the ridge, and the sun burst upon us again. Ahead of us, to the north-east, rose the seven-thousand-foot, grass-covered peak of La Moriond. Below us, writhing through the pine woods, was the blue road, La Betone, the Brenner road through Modena to the south. We walked down to it over the velvety grass, feeling very exposed, for just here there were no trees. The best place to cross appeared to be where a few houses clustered at the edge of the road. These, we had found out, contained no Germans. As we approached the road, two girls saw us and ran along to meet us. We hopped across the road like scalded cats, for a lorry was coming up the hill, but the girls called after us and told us to wait. We tried the Italian story first, but then decided they were safe enough. When they heard we were English, they called up to the window of a roadside house, behind which we were standing. Two faces appeared, and two guttural voices wished us good morning in English. They belonged to two South African soldiers from the camp at Modena, who had escaped and been guided by one of their ex-guards, to his home. Here, on the very edge of the principal road from Germany to Rome, they had lived for three weeks.

'We are staying here till the British take Rome,' they said, 'then our host is going to guide us down there.' Such crass stupidity was beyond our comprehension.

We asked the girls for food, and they brought us fresh bread and salami and cheese—almost more than we could carry. Then we scrambled down a muddy path to the next stream, crossed this one also by a mill, and climbed again, through a country of cultivated fields and isolated farms, towards the Libro Aperto.

We ate our lunch on the col at the base of Libro Aperto, in a wood of flamboyant beech trees, rioting in the autumn sunlight, and contrasting with the unblemished blue of the sky. The mountain is well named the Open Book. At its foot lies spread out the whole history of Italian culture. For this is the border of Tuscany again. The range curves away south-eastward, and to the south stretches a green country of pine woods and little 'paggi'—the gentle rounded Tuscan hills—and beyond again the great plain, stretching to the gates of Florence, abounding in vineyards and olive groves and rich cultivation. Up on the ridge to the south-west, behind us now, is the German-occupied hotel of La Betone, a white gash in the dark pines. The main road is a darker line across the trees, zigzagging down from the pass.

We bathed in a little stream in the woods, shaved, slept in the sun for half an hour, and then followed the stream down to the valley, where it joined a river and flowed south-eastward in a deep-wooded fold between the main range and some hills. A good mule track ran along the river's edge, occasionally leaving it to climb some rocky outcrop to a village perched precariously atop. These villages we avoided, keeping always to the river, and meeting no one but washerwomen and cow herds, and the owners of a mill, where we were given bread and apples. And always close to us travelled the great pylons which carried the power from the Alps to Rome. 'Follow the pylons to Rome,' we had been told this morning. But the pylons could go where we couldn't go—through Florence and across the plains to the south.

Eventually the mule track led us to Cotigliano, a town notorious for its population of Fascist spies, according to the locals. Here the main road emerged again from the trees and followed the river, but on the opposite side to us.

About six o'clock we started to look for somewhere to spend the night. There were no isolated farms, so we would have to risk a village. Soon we found a small one, where the river flowed into a reservoir, and the main road passed at a respectable distance on the far side. We called at a mill on the edge of the village, to ask if it was clear of Fascists and Germans.

For the first time I thought we had made a rash mistake. The miller, a young, not very pleasant-looking character, was most suspicious of us. He had all the aspect of the real Fascist. I think he probably was one, but wanted to keep in good odour with both sides. At any rate, after a lot of persuasion he agreed to put us up for the night, and gradually we realised that his behaviour was due mainly to acute fright at having us around. We could not sleep in the mill, so waited there two hours until it was dark, and he could take us safely up to his house.

This miller was a joiner, too. The joiner's shop was on the first floor and the mill below. Upstairs he spent his time making furniture, with all the concentration of the true craftsman, revelling in the skill of his hand and the precision of his tools, and ankle-deep in sweet-smelling sawdust. When the farmers brought their grain to be ground, the sawdust was brushed aside, and the grain tipped on to the floor of the joiner's shop, whence it poured through two holes down to the mill. Inevitably a certain amount of sawdust went down, too. This was good for business: the miller was able to make a little on every sack of grain ground.

This is the perfect vocation: miller cum joiner. You spend your day at your hobby, whose waste products go to swell your flour sacks. Every now and then you move a few levers, setting in motion the massive wheel, and the water then does the work. The only paperwork is filling up an imposing Fascist form, saying how many hours of work you have done that day.

The miller took us to his home for supper. His pretty young wife was equally petrified and eyed us gravely and silently. It was all somewhat embarrassing. Preparations for supper were interesting. She rolled back the tablecloth, and there, spread all over the table like another cloth, was a thick layer of dough— the fruits of the miller's sawdust-substitution. This the girl attacked with a knife, cutting it into long thin strips, which went to make a most beautiful minestrone.

Our sweet seclusion was then rudely broken by the arrival of a most obvious Englishman, dressed in brown tweed coat and plus-fours, much too big for him, and a very smart Homburg. This was Lieutenant Hartigan from one of the other camps. How he managed to get all this way looking like the caricature of the English squire and talking no Italian was beyond our understanding. He treated the Italian family in just that off-hand way the caricature squire would, too. We weren't very pleased to see him.

After supper our host plucked up courage and asked us if we would like to hear the English radio. So we crept furtively through the village street to the house of a friend of his, where we sat for an hour in a miniature kitchen, with the friend and his young wife and our host, drinking wine and listening to Radio London, Radio Algiers, and the German-controlled Radio Roma. The news depressed us. Our armies were hardly advancing at all. We had a very long way yet to walk.

Then about midnight we were led out to a big barn, where we turned in on the top of a huge pile of hay and slept like logs.

### Twenty-third Day

THE ANXIOUS miller called us before dawn. Hartigan was off first and we never saw him again. We climbed the ridge eastwards and stopped in the small village of Spignana to try and get some food. But everyone was scared stiff of us. The cottagers refused even to talk to us. The shop said they had nothing to sell. In desperation we tried the priest, but he was in the middle of Mass. We felt thoroughly outcast as we stalked out of the village, under the furtive glances of peasant women and the angry stare of the large posters, gummed to high walls, announcing that those who helped us would be shot. In fact, we heard later that a man in this district had recently been executed for helping a prisoner—which probably explained their unfriendliness. For this was not at all like our hospitable Tuscany.

We tried again for food at a well-to-do farm, but the padrone said he had nothing, and suggested we call at a miserable hovel, a mile or two farther on, where they might be able to oblige. We walked on and came to the place, a desperately poor-looking cottage in the woods on a steep hillside. And as often happened, the poorest people were the most hospitable, for the two old ladies who owned the place produced polenta and cheese and apples. And we repaid their hospitality by breaking a tumbler.

Then we walked on down into a deep gorge, across a stream, and up an apparently vertical hill, through thick undergrowth. Higher up, we heard the hack-hack of woodcutters, their snatches of song, and occasional shouts, and soon we came upon them, surrounded by an almost impassable stockade of fallen trees. The woodcutters—the carbonari—are akin to the shepherds. Gypsy-like, they live in the high places and fear no man. Their humour and energy are unbounded; they are above the cares of civilised life. They look ferocious, with their charcoal-blackened faces, but they are generosity itself. They haven't the placidity of the shepherd, but all of his exuberance.

Over the brow of this hill we came into a broad valley, with smaller hills and the broad plain visible beyond. The main road to Pistoia ran through the valley, and there were many red-roofed villages and kitchen gardens. It didn't look at all an inviting valley to cross.

We decided to traverse the hillside still towards the southeast, until we came to a suitable place to cross the road. Then began one of the most heartbreaking mornings of all. We were walking through thick woods along the side of the hills, every half-mile or so dipping down into a gully which scored its way down to the valley bottom. In these gullies the undergrowth is practically impenetrable. Sometimes we found little paths, which led us in the wrong direction and then petered out, leaving us in a thicker part of the wilderness than ever. Halfway up a hillside is the very worst place to walk. Either go along the ridge, or in the valley bottom, where the gullies have smoothed out.

About noon our range of hills came to an abrupt end, where a valley cut right across to the north. Under the rim of the hill clung a village—red and white houses and a hotel—and a big metalled road ran through the gap. Beyond, the hills rose again, two thousand feet, to a perfect wilderness of scrub and fir plantation and rocky outcrop. Now we should have to cross one of these roads.

We were walking down towards the village, when suddenly, in front of us, coming up the path, we saw two men in shirtsleeves, with big rucksacks. They were only a hundred yards ahead and saw us at the same moment. There was no hiding. The first man came up and addressed us in French: 'Etes-vous anglais?' My stomach felt empty and my heart thumped. I thought of the Fascist bands of the 'M' Division, searching the countryside for prisoners.

After a few uncomfortable moments, he went on to explain that he was an officer in the Italian Air Force, who had run away to escape the Germans, and who was now endeavouring to form a band of guerillas up in the macchia. He was very earnest that we should join him and help to round up the many British troops who were wandering aimlessly about. He convinced us of his genuineness, and we were impressed by his common sense and keenness. We decided to stay a day with them to find out more and to give us time to have our shoes repaired.

So the four of us turned round and climbed the path to the high ridge, up into a plantation of young firs, remote from any civilisation, and providing a first-class hide-out. This was 'la macchia'—the maquis, the wilderness, the traditional country for partisans. Here you could defy an army for months, hiding in the undergrowth by day, making quick raids on the nearby roads by night, never staying in the same place.

These two impressed their personality deeply upon us. Terente Gusmano was small and blond and blue-eyed. He had a hard efficiency, unnatural in an Italian. His brain was fertile and orderly, considering the smallest thing, weighing chances, planning ahead. His companion, Beppe, was a countryman, tall, hatchet-faced, silent—the typical mountain guide, versed in all the lore of the country. And each, in his own way, was fiercely burning with patriotism and hatred of the German. That was a fact which hit you between the eyes: so unlike the usual melodramatic Italian boasts of patriotism and partisan-feeling.

Presently Gusmano told us to halt, while he and Beppe went cautiously on, walking a hundred yards apart. Gusmano stopped in the bushes at the next corner, and Beppe went on alone. We waited minutes in the immense stillness of the mountains, listening for Beppe's whistle to say all was clear. Then on we went again and soon came to a small log cabin, concealed among the trees near a spring. This was an old Milizia Forestale hut, deserted now by its owners, but occupied, we found, by three British officers and a sergeant from the Fontanellata camp. They, like us, had met Gusmano, and were staying a few days here to see what the form was. They hid in the macchia by day, coming into the hut for their meals, which Beppe or Gusmano brought each day, and sleeping there at night on the wide wooden couch.

We were not attracted by them. They seemed to have surprisingly little initiative and expected everything done for them.

Beppe unpacked the rucksacks. There was fresh bread and mutton, cheese, salami, and fruit, and a bottle of red wine. We set to at once, excited by the sight of real meat again.

Over lunch we heard more of Gusmano's plan. He reckoned there were a thousand soldiers hereabouts, hiding in the macchia, almost an entire regiment, led by their own colonel. They were scattered now but could be collected in a short time. Their trouble was lack of arms, explosives and food. Gusmano was the colonel's able lieutenant who had undertaken to get these things. He had thought his plan out thoroughly. Some of his guerillas had been enlisted in the German forces, so-called Fascists, and were now driving German transport. They were running the length of Tuscany, sometimes even down to Rome, stealing arms and bringing them back under the piles of provisions or stores they officially transported for the Germans. Others were collecting food and storing it in the mountains, for Gusmano realised that as soon as they started operating, the villagers—unlike the Slav villagers—would be too frightened to give food or help in any way. Other men had gone off to contact a British wireless set rumoured to be operating in the neighbourhood, and an envoy had been sent down to cross the lines and contact the British, with a view to having arms and equipment dropped for them by parachute. It all sounded very thorough and intelligent, and was worth further investigation. If they could make it a going concern, and we could collect a few hundred British soldiers, we might be able to do considerable damage to the German communications. For it was a perfect strategic position, in wild country, but within easy reach of four big roads which came down through the Apennines from

Germany, snaking through passes and gorges over viaducts—beautiful country for sabotage. And from this hut we could see, all day long, the supply transports moving south, along the road below, feeding the life to Kesselring's distant army.

At any rate we agreed to wait and see. Beppe arranged to put us up at another hut about four hours' walk away on the mountain, beyond the village of Maresca. So after lunch we walked down again by the path we had come. But when we got to the brow of the slope looking down into Maresca below, they decided it would be unsafe for us to pass through the village in daylight. Gusmano told us to lie up here in the undergrowth until dark, when they would fetch us. And he would bring us tea at four o'clock.

'But we don't want tea,' we said.

'Oh yes, you must have tea.'

So Frank and I slept in the sun, until we were called by a low whistle, and there was Gusmano with a rucksack full of more meat and fresh bread and fruit and wine. This was ridiculous. We hadn't fed so well in years. We arranged a rendezvous on the edge of the village for eight o'clock, and he left us.

The sun set, and a hard blue sky slowly paled to a soft grey, and a chill breeze stirred through the bracken. Frank and I collected our things and walked down to the stream at the edge of the village. At precisely eight o'clock two shapes loomed up out of the dark. We had a moment of panic, for we didn't know the little short one, but then we recognised Beppe's bulk, dressed now in a smooth lounge suit. The little man was introduced as Signor Viparelli, the hotel proprietor who supplied all the food.

We crept through the village with the stealth of Red Indians to a farm on the further edge. Here a girl appeared out of the dark and led us to a big hay barn. We went inside. Beppe produced a torch and relieved us of our matches, so that we shouldn't set the hay afire. Then they left us to get the supper. After a while Viparelli returned with Gusmano and another monster meal of meat and bread and wine. So much meat would make us ill! We ate by torchlight, while Viparelli talked in quiet whispers, pregnant with suppressed excitement and anti-German fervour. He quite made my blood stir, and I felt intrigued to be included in such a gorgeous conspiracy.

At last they said good night, gave us each a pair of boots, and left with our disreputable ones for repair. We turned in under the hay and slept with full-bellied content.

Air battle: 24 Fortresses—6 fighters. 1 Fortress hit. Perfect formation.

### Twenty-fourth Day

BEPPE called us long before dawn, with another big meal. We had to go out through the chestnut woods, clumping up the path in our enormous borrowed mountain boots, to lie up for the day. We found a secluded corner in a dry stream bed and settled down to pass fourteen boring hours. It was cold. An inquisitive wind prowled round every corner, so that we couldn't find a lee. About midday, for an hour, the sun shone on us, through a gap in the chestnut canopy, but for the rest of the time we were in dark shadow. I was miserable with a new crop of boils erupting all over my right hip and buttock. Frank was in delightful mood, as he always was at the most trying times. He fished out of his rich imagination the most fantastic stories, mostly about his more peculiar relations, doing his best to keep me cheerful. I should be a bad shipmate in a boatload of survivors. I like to suffer boredom in silence, and can do so without getting demoralised, but I can't turn on the gallant stuff to bolster the morale of others. Frank is wonderful at this. He'd keep a gang of Lascars happy on a desert island. His descriptions of the Abyssinian campaign, usually with a trend towards the ridiculous in the Italian, were brilliant.

After interminable hours, during which our only excitement

was a visit from some children collecting chestnuts, Viparelli arrived with lunch. Gusmano was spending the day with his wife, he said; Beppe had gone off to guide the other Englishmen across the valley and our boots were not yet done. We should have to wait another day. We said we would like to spend the night in a house where we could get a bath, and he said he might manage to get us into the hotel.

The day wore on. The sun set and we got even colder. There was no tea this afternoon, but lunch had been more than enough. About eight-thirty Beppe arrived, very tired after his long day's walk, to guide us into the hotel. We set off like Red Indians in single file, creeping from tree to tree, pausing to listen, making detours, laying false tracks and doubling back. His thoroughness was a revelation. After a bewildering half-hour of this, in the pitch-dark night, we suddenly arrived at the back door of the Pensione Maresca. Beppe went in to contact Viparelli, and a minute or two later we were beckoned in, across the hall, and up the stairs to the second floor. The hotel is a seasonal one, empty at this time of year. On the second floor Viparelli had prepared a double room for us—feather beds and all—and there a dinner table was laid for two with more cutlery on it than I had seen since before the war.

Soon Signora Viparelli, a large motherly woman, bustled in with a big bowl of minestra. We sat down at the little table, with its white cloth and napkins, and fell to ravenously. There seemed something incongruous in eating such a homely dish in such an elegant manner. Then followed veal cutlets, and vegetables, and salad, with a bottle of white wine. Then a delicious sweet and coffee. No guest at the Pensione Maresca could ever have fed better or with more exquisite service. Signor Viparelli himself served the wine with all the gravity and subservience of the head waiter at Claridge's. It was all rather ridiculous but delightful.

With the coffee came Signor and Signora Viparelli and a

fugitive Italian soldier who was staying with them, to ensconce themselves in comfortable chairs and talk to us. The soldier was typical of the sort of thing that was happening in Italy. A deserter from his unit, unable to get through to his German-occupied home, he had asked for work from the hotel-keeper and been accepted. Now he cut the wood and washed the dishes, and was fed and looked after as one of the family. His passport to such hospitality was his fanaticism. For Viparelli himself was a fanatical communist. Like Beppe, like Gusmano, there was something frightening in the intensity of his feelings—something I had only met before in Yugoslavs. The perfect partisan type. Viparelli was perhaps more an anarchist than a communist. He wanted to do away with all authority. Why couldn't we all live equally—equal pay, equal say, equal opportunity? And yet there was something amusing in the simplicity of his ideas. To him this blissful state of life could be produced without any trouble or pain to anyone. He couldn't understand what was holding it up. Behind his apparent fanaticism was a childlike friendliness to all things, and complete enslavement to the present feudal system. He was the perfect waiter and liked it.

About eleven o'clock they produced a big tin bath and cans of boiling water. We shaved and bathed, and then turned in in the exquisite beds. This would be another night to remember: sleeping in the best hotel in Maresca, as guests of the proprietor.

### Twenty-fifth Day

OUR TALK last night with Viparelli had decided us to go on. We were sure enough of their genuineness as partisans, but the task of collecting arms and supporters looked like being a long one. We had no intention of hanging around for some weeks, spending the days in the Tiger country, and the nights in various barns, eventually to be pawns in an Italian game. Rather would we hope to get through the lines and send them arms by air.

Viparelli and the soldier took us out into the woods before

dawn, so we only had four hours' sleep in luxury. At breakfast-time Gusmano and Beppe arrived, and we told them of our plans. Surprisingly, they didn't seem sorry now to hear we were going.

They went away and later returned with clothes and money, and much food, and our shoes repaired. We offered to pay, but they wouldn't hear of it, saying the organisation was well financed, and part of its job was helping British prisoners. I was quite sorry to say goodbye to them. We couldn't have been treated more generously, or our needs administered to more thoroughly. We had arranged signs between our aircraft and the partisans, and dropping areas for supplies and men, and three weeks later I passed the information on to our Intelligence in Bari, who seemed interested. I hope that Gusmano and his guerrillas received the help they needed and inflicted suitable damage on the Germans, for such faith and energy deserved to be rewarded.

Beppe led us out of the wood and set us on our way. We set off eastwards, traversing the hillside, across small meadows, and through more oak woods. A little child of four shouted after us: 'Look out, the Germans will get you.' We felt very gauche at being recognised by one so young.

We were pretty close to civilisation now. In the valley bottom to our right was a big munitions factory with its satellite workers' villages. On the hilltops were flat towers and observation posts, which made us feel somewhat uneasy. Two big main roads converged in the valley and swept eastwards, paralleled by a railway, which somehow we had to cross.

Fortune was with us, though, for we found a place where the valley narrowed, with the woods reaching down to the road on either side. The road and railway were deserted just then, and it took but a moment to cross them both, cross the stream by a bridge, and disappear again in the woods beyond.

Here the country got wilder. We followed a mule track

up a long valley towards the ridge, through pine trees, where the carbonari were working, ferrying their loads of logs down on the long sagging wire cables, shouting to each other across the valley. It was raining now, and the carpet of pine needles smelled delicious.

Topping the hill, we looked down southward to a broad plain, in which lay Pistoia.

Through the rain we could see the maze of railway lines weaving into the city, and the airfield. Eastwards, on the next height of the range, was the Futa road, another of the main arteries, which here burst through the Apennines, joining Germany with the south. It snaked down from the high Futa pass, through pine and scrub to Pistoia below. This road, too, we had to cross. So we turned eastwards again, preferring to follow the mountains and cross it in the wild country.

It was evening by the time we approached the road, climbing upwards to it through the scrub, feeling uncomfortably exposed. Convoys rumbled down it, and occasionally staff cars whizzed down or hummed laboriously up. Beyond, the country looked infinitely wild, with not a sign of habitation. Then we came upon a band of disreputable carbonari, with pitch-black faces and flashing eyes and teeth, clothed in dilapidated sacking to keep out the rain. We asked them if there was a farm close by, where we could stay the night, telling them just who we were. They were on their way home, and agreed to show us to the only available farm. They, themselves, would have put us up, but they lived in a village in the plain, and only yesterday the Fascists had caught some prisoners-of-war in the village. They had wanted to shoot them, but they had been rescued by the Germans and taken off to Florence in a staff car.

We approached the house, and one of the carbonari went ahead to contact the farmer. Soon they returned together, the farmer shaking his head and apologising profusely that he couldn't put us up. His house was on the edge of the Futa road. Yesterday the Germans had been billeted there, while they mined the road; they might come again tomorrow.

He gave us a small piece of bread, but no advice, and we wandered on to the road, very wet and miserable, and not quite knowing where we were going to spend the night. So different from the Pensione Maresca.

Crossing the road was a tricky business. We expected sentries to be guarding the mines, so approached like good boy scouts, through the trees. Frank slipped across and all seemed well. Then I ran across, and as we clambered up the far bank a motor cyclist turned the corner, leading down an interminable convoy, which stretched, in labyrinthine coils, right up to the Futa—big covered lorries nose to tail, but no guns or tanks. The noise of them sounded like the roar of breakers on the shore, as they crept down in bottom gear, heading for Florence and the front line.

We breathed again. Crossing roads was never a genial business. But we were no nearer a home for the night. We wandered on in the dark and the rain. The country appeared appallingly desolate. Then we came on a small road, winding upwards off the main road, and followed it, but found no houses. At last we spotted the shadow of a building and found it to be an empty cowshed, devoid of any straw, or even doors, with open slits in its stone walls. This at least was shelter, so we decided to make the best of it.

There was nothing dry with which to make a fire, and, anyway, the light of a fire might have been risky. Frank put the bread down somewhere and we couldn't even find it with the light of a candle, however much we searched, so that was the end of our supper. We took off our wet clothes and put on our spare ones, which were almost as wet, from the rolled-up blanket. Then we climbed into the narrow manger, which would just take us end to end with our knees bent, and put the wet blanket over our two heads in the middle. The last thing we did was to eat some halibut tablets from Frank's precious emergency store. Their effect was astonishing. We felt quite a glow of heat almost immediately, and actually both fell asleep.

### Twenty-sixth Day

IT WAS a dismal awakening in that cowshed. The rain was coming down in buckets, and the wind whistled in through the cracks in the wall. The only consolation was that by the daylight we were able to locate the bread—in the middle of the floor.

We walked along the road. It appeared to be a lonely track, deserted except for the passage of one lorry, whose tyre marks we saw in the soft gravel. It wandered along the side of the hills through a forest reserve of pines. Even here, and in spite of large notices, the trees had been cut down in huge areas. The ground in these areas looked sour and burnt, a brown scar in the green texture, livid with the harsh wrinkles of erosion. This is the face of Italy, being devastated foot by foot through the short-sighted stupidity of the population.

We came on a colony of carbonari, inhabiting little igloos of piled faggots, turfed outside. Smoke came through a hole in the roof of each of these igloos, and as we approached and were seen innumerable children and old hags and a few old men started crawling out through the low hole that served as a door, looking like bees leaving a hive. There was a smell of cooking food, but when we asked for something to eat they refused. They were strange, foreign-looking creatures, like gypsies, sullen and distrustful.

We walked on, until the road came to a sudden end at a rather smart rest-home, made of wooden boards and thatched, with a balcony all round, chalet style. This was the rest-house of the Milizia Forestale. We went in and asked for a drink and some food. These were produced, without any particular enthusiasm, by a young woman and her small child. We had a good meal, fresh milk, then wine and bread and cheese. Then in came her husband, one of the Milizia in plain clothes. He gave us some good advice. He told us that most of the Milizia were Mussolini's men and were working for the Germans. They were the people to beware of, for it was they who knew every path in the mountains, and would be likely to be on the prowl looking for escaped prisoners. The Germans themselves never dared go off the main roads. The man was very nervous and gave the impression that he, too, felt he ought to arrest us, but as he was all alone he didn't like to try, so we did not linger long.

The road had been one of our best friends, leading us straight in the way we wanted to go, without much uphill work, but now we were forced by the line of the hills to enter a deep, narrow, wooded valley running north-eastwards. We followed a narrow path, churned into a bog by the feet of many sheep, along the edge of a stream. There were tiny villages in this valley, just a few houses each, clustered at the water's edge, with a few kitchen gardens cut out of the forest. In one of them we were invited in for food and to dry ourselves at the fire.

These people were quite different from our previous acquaintances of the day. They were delighted to see Englishmen.

Several of them spoke English. Huge slabs of polenta were pressed upon us, with urgent cries of 'Mangia, mangia'. We stripped off the wettest of our clothes and contrived to warm ourselves a bit. It was too early yet to make our lunchtime halt, so we decided to go on shortly, and this decision was reinforced by the arrival of more British prisoners,—rather disappointing, just as we thought we were off the beaten track. It was not that we disliked our own kin, but we were always frightened that a regular escape route might be watched, and we endeavoured, as far as possible, to keep away from the more obvious places.

Our hospitable friends told us that in a village a little further on was a South African Army doctor, staying in a farm, so I decided to visit him professionally for my boils. By now they were in an appalling mess. The whole of my right buttock had become one eruption which stuck to my shirt, was painful when I walked, and agony when I tried to sit down.

A mile or two farther on we came to the village of Mosca. It consisted of but two farmhouses, close together on the edge of the wood, about a hundred yards above the river. Here, in the larger one, we met the doctor and a South African friend of his. They were living en famille, in the greatest comfort, paying for their keep by working in the fields with the peasants. The doctor had even worked up a small practice among the valley people. He told us enthusiastically that his best case was a mastoid. There seemed to be no inducement for them to go on, though they said they were only waiting for their host to buy them some boots. This sort of thing was happening everywhere. POWs were settling down quite content for the war to come to them.

Most of them seemed oblivious to the fact that it was only a question of time before the Germans found them out, or the peasants, bored with them, or frightened, threw them out. Many must have been recaptured through this short-sighted and indolent attitude.

However, the doctor was a godsend to me just now. He said that there was only one thing for me to do—stay in bed for ten days until the whole thing had cleared up. When we told him we couldn't afford to do that, he fixed me a truss from a long bandage, to keep the boils clear of my clothes. We had lunch with the good farmer, took a tracing of the South African's excellent road-map, and said goodbye to them.

We walked down to the river, crossed it by a bridge, and climbed the long hill on the southern side of the valley. The rain had stopped now, the sun was bursting through, I felt more comfortable.

Over the next ridge we saw before us another steep-sided valley, with the blue road snaking down it from Bologna to Florence, and clusters of red and white villages along its course. Walking down to it, through the chestnut woods, we realised that we should about reach it at the end of our day's walk, and that certainly would be no place to stay the night. The road was continually busy with German transport, and some of those roadside houses were possibly occupied by the Hun. We decided then to stop in a small village called Lucciana, for there were no isolated farms here. Lucciana was on the near slope of the valley, looking down to the river, and up to the road on the far slope.

We stopped a peasant outside the village, and learnt from him that there were no Germans or Fascists in the place. Then we called at a fairly large house on the edge of the village. But the wife turned us away in fear, making excuses that her husband was not at home, and recommended we try at a miserably poor farmhouse a few yards below. By this time we were so wet and tired, and my boils were so painful, that we reckoned any place would do, and the nearer the better. So we called there, and were immediately welcomed by the two old ladies who owned the place.

We sat in front of the fire while they washed and dried and mended our clothes. Frank brought out the photograph of his nephew and told the usual story of how it was his small son that he had never seen. I told my usual sob-stuff about not having seen 'mama mia' for seven years (which was almost true). Those two white lies never failed to win us sympathy, and usually brought forth instantaneous food and drink, and many tearful expressions of 'poveretti' and gasps of motherly delight at the sight of Frank's lovely 'bambino'.

Then the meal was produced—one of the best we had ever had, steaming minestrone and bread and cheese and wine. The room was marvellously warm, and the reaction after a long day was terrific. So much so that I fainted in the middle of supper and had to be revived with more wine and cries of 'poverino'. And their hospitality included a bed.

### Twenty-seventh Day

WE LEFT at seven o'clock to cross the Bologna road before the traffic got too great. Down through the vineyards to the torrent, across it by a big bridge, where the main road crossed, and up into the undergrowth on the far side. Past an austere-looking 'Palazzo' on a little hill—where we heard there were British prisoners staying—and so up towards the next ridge.

Climbing this long slope, we overtook a man and his wife trudging up, overburdened with suitcases and bundles. After talking to them for a bit, we admitted we were English, reckoning to be safe in this wild country, and decided to walk with them.

He was a factory worker from Florence, a typical politically minded factory worker of the sort that either become Communists or Fascists. This one was a Fascist. His mind was still poisoned with the Mussolini canker. He quoted all the usual newspaper phrases about demo-plutocratic-Judaism. He nattered about living space and colonies and war guilt. He was the sort with which it is useless to argue, but we enjoyed doing so, because he was far too timid ever to report us.

They were evacuating Florence, and going to live with his wife's parents in a farm in the hills. Florence had been bombed by the Americans. Not a factory had been hit, he said, but one of the more populous living quarters had been razed to the last house. No wonder he was unsympathetic to us. And yet in a way he was polite and helpful. He offered to show us the route and asked us home for a meal. Underneath the bad-mannered Fascist you could glimpse the natural courtesy of the Italian peasant—snatched from the land but a few years before to earn better pay and live in worse conditions in some Florentine slum.

We left them in the mountains, and slowly descended to the wide rich plain north of Florence. Away to the south, we could see the smoke of the city, and the hills beyond. Here, chestnut woods gave way to meadows and idle brooks, and then to the fertile fields and vineyards of the plain. We could abandon now the steep mountain paths, forever going in the wrong direction, and set a compass course dead straight across the plain. Over plough, through apple orchards, through vineyards where the vines climbed vigorously up trees, instead of being stunted and close-packed on their terraces, as in the mountain vineyards; and between the trees vegetables were planted. The plain undulated gently into the blue, sparkling distance. Sometimes the hilltops—the little Tuscan 'poggi'—were decorated with small woods, or elegant palazzi in a cluster of cypress trees. This was the picture book Tuscany, sweltering in humid sunlight, abundant with all the good things of nature. There was indeed a fat opulence about the scene. The farms were sleek and well-kept, the orchards were neat, the cattle looked deliberately well-to-do. And the peasants were pleasantly incurious.

In the mountains everyone wants to know who you are, where you are going and why. Here we walked—two strangers—straight across their fields, plucking their apples and tomatoes as we went, and all the interest the straw-hatted, shirt-sleeved farmers took in us was to wish us good day. Yes, there was infinite joy for us here in the plain.

As dusk closed in, we were close to the north of Borgo San Lorenzo, where the railway sweeps north across a great brick viaduct. We came upon the railway suddenly, as we turned out of a farmyard on to a small lane. There, not twenty yards away, were two Milizia men guarding a bridge where the railway crossed the lane. We just had time to double back into the farmyard before they turned round. Thereafter, we had to tackle the railway more cautiously, hiding in the bushes alongside the line and spying out the land before sneaking across the rails.

A mile or two beyond the railway we came to a farm, and decided to ask for shelter for the night. There was a woman in the yard feeding the chickens or something. We went up and asked her. She got a bit of a shock, poor thing, seeing two strange shapes in the dusk, asking for lodging, and the reception didn't look too friendly at first. However, she took us in, allowed us to wash at the kitchen sink, and said she would ask the padrone about it.

Shortly after there was a sound outside of oxen being put to bed, and then in came the men back from work. Our reception from them was quite different. They were delighted to see us. The padrone, Signor Borselli, quite a young man, welcomed us with open arms and a wealth of hospitality, quite unknown to the more dour mountain folk with whom we were more familiar.

The men—there were four of them—removed their big boots caked with the rich red valley mud, washed and put on their coats, all the while talking to us from the other end of the room in ecstatic voices, obviously tickled to death at having such visitors. Then we moved in to supper in the parlour. It was obviously a special meal for us. A white cloth was on the table, glasses, cutlery and flasks of wine. The room, hung with monstrous pictures of the Borselli ancestors, and faded agricultural diplomas, and lurid pictures of the Virgin and Child, looked as though it was seldom used.

The six of us sat down, and the woman brought in the meal. First, there was an immense bowl of the usual minestrone. Our plates were overloaded. We emptied them and had them refilled. Our protests were overridden with cries of 'Mangia, mangia' and 'Favorisca'. Then in came a special meat dish just for Frank and me. Then bread and cheese. And always glass after glass of exquisite wine. We got rather flushed and intoxicated, not so much with the wine as with the whole Bacchanalian generosity of the feast.

After the meal we sat and talked. The women, who had had their meal round the kitchen fire, edged into the room and stood silently and excitedly in the background, listening. We heard of Borselli's first introduction to British prisoners of war.

There had been a big troops' camp at Florence. At the armistice, the Italian commandant had opened the gates and let them out. Four of them had stayed a few nights with the Borsellis, and then decided for some reason to return to the camp, where, of course, they were captured by the Germans. But many had remained at large and were now reported to be hiding in a big wood north of Florence, fed and armed by the local population. Borselli had enjoyed having them, but they were uneducated fellows, he said, and couldn't supply him with the interesting conversation that we could.

Religion came up for discussion.

'Are you Christians or Anglicans?' asked one young man.

'Anglicans, but Anglicans are Christians.'

'That's impossible. They don't believe in the Holy Virgin.'

'Nonsense,' said Borselli, who posed as a man of the world, and wanted to help us out of a difficulty. 'Of course they are Christians.'

This was a popular belief in rural Italy; that no one but Catholics were Christians. We avoided this sort of conversation when possible, for we always bumped up against Roman dogmatism. In this case we steered the conversation into a channel which always intrigued them—the fact that Anglican priests could marry. Borselli considered it very broad-minded and sensible. The women in the shadows giggled and looked embarrassed.

Inevitably the war came up. They were quite prepared to listen to anything we had to say. There was no pride in any of the much-vaunted Italian achievements in the early days of the war. We told them the truth about Matapan, and Libya, and Tunis. They listened and lapped it up with astonished cries of 'Accidente!'

Then we came back to this farm of theirs. And now Borselli talked as a man with no cares. The land was his life. Here on the plain the land never let you down. There was always abundance of everything. Even requisitioning and the quota couldn't make any difference, for they could always conceal half of it. No one in the valley farms ever went short. The laws had to be appeased, of course, but after that you fed yourselves like fighting cocks, and sold the rest for fabulous prices on the black market. This eternal plenty affected the whole character of the valley folk. They were placid and sensual, with a breadth and depth to their generosity. In the mountains there was something fierce about the hospitality. 'We live by the grace of God and the sweat of our brow. What little we glean you may share with us.' The mountain man could tighten his belt and live indefinitely on his determination. The valley man was soft and would crack, but for the moment he was the jollier type to meet.

This was the most delightful conversation we ever had. I could have gone on talking all night. It was surprising with what fluency Italian came to me when I was really interested. Borselli was thrilled, too, to have two Englishmen to whom he could talk and by whom he could be understood.

But even the best conversations must end, and we had to sleep if we were to move on early the next day. We went upstairs to bed about eleven o'clock.

The first floor of the farmhouse was huge, for it covered the stables as well. There was a long wide landing of bare planks, with about six rooms heading off each side. Frank and I shared a room with Borselli and his nephew. We shared one double bed and they the other. We went to sleep feeling just like members of the family.

*This is as far as Peter Medd was able to write his own story from his notes, before his death: it is the diary of his companion, Frank Simms, which takes it up and completes it.*

# PART TWO

By Frank Simms

### *Twenty-eighth Day*

WE HAD breakfast, of coffee and milk and bread, in the parlour. There was a picture of the Borselli crest on one wall. 'The family had not always been peasants,' said the man in the panama hat; 'once they had been military chaplains and even officers.'

The room also had a picture, an old German engraving of a scene in a wine cellar. The only picture hung purely for its aesthetic value, I saw. There were also ones of the royal family and Badoglio. The Borsellis gave us a length of cord before we left to do our bundle up properly.

We walked along the plain a little further and began to climb. In front of us was a cart with a man and a woman in it. We reached a village where we were asked into a house for wine. The son of the house was a prisoner in Egypt, and we assured them that he would be getting lots to eat. They imagined England was next door to Egypt—otherwise they couldn't see why they and we should fight there. It being Sunday, preparations were being made for lunch. The table was covered with a sheet of dough from which little squares were cut, a lump of potato put in the middle and the corners folded on it. This is how ravioli is made.

The people who had been in the cart in front of us had now put it in a shed and were now driving the horse up the track, which had narrowed considerably. When we reached their village we met the man who asked us into his house for lunch. We had minestrone, stewed chicken, and then fried birds. I didn't ask what they were, in case I found they were larks. The village where we were hoping to pass the night was called Londa. We walked down through a lot of chestnut-wooded hills, past a village and across a road. The grapes were being gathered for the vendemmia, which was very late round here. At one house, where everyone was filling the baskets with grapes, we were given some, and then asking for water, were shown into the kitchen. The woman of the house was an Egyptian married to an Italian, and soon we were chattering away in Arabic.

We should perhaps have stayed there, as they had a duck and a rabbit ready for the vendemmia supper, and we might have trod in the winepress. The first pressing is still done by foot, and then when the bulk has been reduced, the grapes are transferred to a metal press. Outside all the houses at this time of year are the maroon heaps of pressed grape-skins with their acrid smell. We soon got lost—the track divided and we took the wrong fork.

We came out on a very high hill in a forestry reserve, with not a house in sight, and ate some bread and tomatoes on the top, then went down the hill, which was very eroded and steep; but to avoid being benighted on such going, we leapt down from rock to rock, like chamois. As it got dark, we reached two isolated houses where we had supper and slept the night in a hay barn.

### Twenty-ninth Day

AFTER a breakfast of bread, wines and grapes, we started off in the direction of Stia. We had on our list a monastery called Eremo, but we got directions on the road that this was out of our way, and we would do better to go to another called La Verna, where they were very good to fugitives. The track we were following was joined by others, and eventually became a road, but as there was nothing but tracks behind us we continued to follow it, though not without a feeling of trepidation, into the outskirts of Stia itself. This was unpleasant, as it was a bigger town than we had expected, with several factories, and workmen on cycles kept on passing us on their way back from their midday meal. We had also been told earlier that three British officers had been denounced by a harlot here earlier in the week. It was true they had been, rather foolishly, stopping the night in an hotel on the main road.

A labourer, coming out of a vineyard, held up two big bunches of grapes for us from his laden barrow, which we ate with relish and refreshment on the hot day.

Finding a path out of the town, which was dominated by a huge castle on a hill, we asked a girl: 'How far to La Verna?' and she replied: 'Six hours.' Later, a man told us it was only two hours off. We asked at a house where there were six Sicilian soldiers escaped from France, making their way home. The owner pointed out our way up a road across the Arno (we were past Florence now) and then south. He didn't know where the monastery was, but thought it not far off. Italians will seldom admit ignorance when giving directions, yet over a distance of more than ten kilos they are very vague.

We walked up the road which was blocked with ox-carts drawn by the beautiful white oxen of Italy, and which were being filled with baskets of grapes. Not feeling very happy on the road, we left it and walked beside the infant Arno, washing our feet in its classic waters. After a false start, the track led upwards amongst a series of almost Alpine meadows, and then we came to the crest. Here there were two passes, and while we were wondering which to take we heard a woodcutter at work a long way off, and went over to him.

Before he would give us the direction, he insisted on our finishing off the bread and wine remaining from his lunch.

Once over the ridge, we crossed a road and skirted the town of Maggiore. Like all these Tuscan towns, it looked beautiful and romantic from without—the crumbling keep, the traces of a wall, and the towers of the churches, all lent it enchantment in the late evening light.

We wanted to stop a little further on, for below us was a main road. Some peasants said we could go back with them to the village, and after a long wait we all moved off. It was only a quarter of a mile from the main road, which was another point against it. When we got there, the man in charge left us outside the barn and said he would send our supper out to us.

After a few minutes a young ex-soldier, still in his uniform, asked us in.

The vendemmia supper was about to be held. We were given seats at one end of the long kitchen by the door. On either side of the fireplace, sitting like a king and queen, on the step level with the fire, were a well-dressed couple we had passed in the dusk. But they were either too proud or too nervous to be seen talking to us, and graciously they patronised the peasant and his wife. 'Twelve to supper; what a beautiful Italian family!'

We had our supper in the kitchen amongst the servants and the farmhands and the children; a good supper of minestrone, fried meat and mashed potatoes with plenty of wine. The whole scene of the long table, with flasks of wine, the great open wood fire, and the ceiling thick with maize cobs, made a good setting for a feast.

We slept that night in a barn, where I was woken up once by a rat jumping on me.

### Thirtieth Day

IT WAS early when we were woken up by the family coming in to work the chaff-cutter. When we had done up our bundles, we went to the house to say goodbye, but really to cadge some breakfast of bread and grapes and wine.

We crossed some water meadows and then began a long, long climb, mostly up a road which everyone said was not used by Fascists or Germans. It was still some way to La Verna, and we did not reach it till two o'clock. A monastery, we felt, would be not only hospitable but clean. There would be good home-grown food, perhaps liqueurs. We would stop the night there and find a cobbler monk who would mend my shoes; the patches on the soles were almost off again. We would dine in a peaceful refectory and sleep in a cool, whitewashed cell, with a charming abbot to talk to us. At last we came in sight of the monastery. A wooded cliff rose sheer from the top of the crest, already fairly high, and the buildings clung precariously to its side. It was here St. Francis received the stigmata. The path began to be marked by huge wooden crosses. An electric-light cable ran beside us. We came to the village which was full of 'monastery' picture postcards and restaurants; there still seemed quite a number of tourists about. We went up a steep ramp, past a statue of the founder with a boy and a pigeon. A man called out to us: 'Whatever you do, don't say you're English.' This was rather upsetting. We went below the towering wall and knocked on the door marked 'Strangers'. After a while a large number of Italian soldiers in ordinary clothes came out, one with a touring-club map from which we copied another list of villages. Among them was an English soldier. A small boy came out and looked at us and remarked: 'Two more,' in a rather impertinent way and disappeared.

Leaning against the wall was a ragged Apollo; he had a pure classic profile and his blond hair, unbrushed, had formed itself into the tight rings of a classic statue. He was a Yugoslav officer, a gymnastic instructor from Belgrave. He lunched at the monastery daily. The boy came down and took us—no refectory, no abbot—to a dirty panelled room with a woman sitting by the fire—the tramps' dining-room. Here, a fat, rather jolly-looking monk brought us a small carafe of wine each, a piece of bread, a plate of rice and some cold beetroot and mushrooms. He twice pinched my cheek, although I hadn't shaved for a week and had, like Peter, grown a moustache. Peter was on the other side of the table, against the wall. There was no cobbler; they didn't put anyone up for the night for fear of German reprisals.

The monastery, by and large, had been a disappointment. A further supply of Italian soldiers came in, and after a few jokes about the reward for us, they gave me a copy of a new pamphlet, and we left.

The whole sole of my left shoe was now loose at the edge and in danger of coming off. We entered the next village and found there were two cobblers; the first was shut and in the other was a Carabinieri, so we didn't stop until lower down for a bathe and a shave at a stream, and I washed my socks. The temperature was much colder than usual and we realised that summer was over.

We halted rather early—we were having an easy day—in a village above Capresi. There were only three houses in it. It was particularly full of flies, dogs, cats and chickens, though the pigs were generally chivvied out of the houses.

For supper we had polenta, one slice of which was covered in cheese, and bread. I was very hungry, and was glad when, after dinner, a big tin of boiled chestnuts was passed round while we talked. This was the first attempt at sociability we found in a poor family after meals. It may have been due to the younger son of the house who had fled from Rome. He must have been a good Fascist once. He had a little supply of luxuries and made himself some coffee with sugar, a great rarity. He never offered any to his mother or his sister who had made the polenta for him, nor did he offer a cigarette to his father, who had an ember in his pipe, nor to his brother. Later, when he washed his hands, he carefully brought down a big piece of scented soap for his own use and took it upstairs afterwards. He did let me use it, though. He had been a waiter in the station restaurant.

That night we slept in the hay loft, which was very warm, being over the cowshed.

### Thirty-first Day

WE STARTED again as soon as the sun was up, and stopped at a big house to ask for bread. While the mistress went to get us some, we looked into another room where two maids were sorting apples. One of them slipped us half a loaf, and the mistress gave us half a loaf. But hers was not of such good quality as the maid's, yet both, I imagine, were made at home.

We ate our breakfast behind a hedge and then passed along a steep path on the edge of a ravine. Here, we passed four Englishmen, but though we exchanged greetings, we did not discover if they were officers or not. We followed a third-class road for a while until our nerves got the better of us and we found a track running parallel to a river. We stopped in a tomato patch and asked the owner if we could pick a few. I showed him my shoe and he said: 'Why, any peasant could do that for you.' This was true; nearly all peasants have their own lasts and do their own minor repairs. If we had known about this earlier, Peter might have been able to save his original English shoes.

We then came to the Tiber, wide and stony, with a shallow clear stream. We stopped to drink from it and to send a rude message to the Imperial City. We crossed where the valley was dominated by a high hill, shaped like a pyramid, with a castle on top, a lovely place to lie up in—the home of our imagined Tuscan noblemen. We saw a lot of lorries parked by the courtyard and were told by a farmer's wife that it was requisitioned by the Germans.

We ate our bread, tomatoes and apples and looked at the view; on our right was the Tiber, in front a broad, intensely cultivated valley, with the main road on the left, at the foot of the mountains. By walking five miles across the plain, which was fairly free of houses, we would be able to regain the mountains quickly and make good going. If we turned left, we would be in the mountains in half an hour, but would only do half the distance before nightfall.

We made very good going; our eyes fixed on a distant spur, we followed tracks when they suited and cut across country otherwise. We passed the town of San Selpulchra on our left and crossed the border into Umbria. We had finished with Tuscany.

As we came out of a vineyard, a man on a cycle saw us and called out: 'Venite qui!' (not even the polite form). We halted and he asked where we were from. Peter replied from Piedmont. He asked us where we were going and Peter said to Rome. 'Venite qui.' We now saw that he had a black shirt on, and a more nasty, smarmy-looking Fascist I have never seen. He didn't appear to have a gun, so we continued along the path which was rather soft going. He got off his cycle and pushed it along after us. We turned off into the plough and he continued to call aggressively: 'Venite qui.' We passed behind a square patch of tobacco, and he abandoned his bicycle. Then, realising that he was alone, he started to shout to the peasants working thereabouts to catch us. None of them paid him or us the slightest attention, and when we were out of sight we ran through several patches of tobacco, crossed a railway and the main road just at the edge of the village of San Guistiniano, another secondary road, and then we were back in the safety of the mountains. It was not the spur we had aimed at when we started to cross the plain, but it didn't matter; the Fascist had greatly increased our day's mileage and it would be too late for him to get a party out to catch us.

We went up to the top of the hill, hoping the Fascist would realise that forty pounds had slipped through his fingers. We passed a well-dressed man, with a gun and a dog, going down to the village; and while we were resting, a party of six men came down the hill we had left. Peter thought they were a gang of Fascists and the sportsman had shown them where we had gone. We went on, though, and soon came to some very wild and eroded country. It was bad going, and below us we saw a road with a few houses beside it; beyond it rose another high and rocky ridge. Peter agreed to stop at the very first house. It was quite isolated. The wife gave us some water in a basin on a metal stand, and I washed after Peter. Unfortunately, in trying to wash one foot, I broke the basin. She was very good about

Lieutenant
Commander
Peter Medd

2nd Lieutenant Frank
Simms before the war

The village of Roggio, taken in the 1950s. The arrow indicates the Abrami's house.

The village of Sillico in the 1920s

The Abrami family
just prior to their
departure from
London for Italy.
Frank Abrami is in
shorts on the right.

The Abrami sisters
after the war
L to R: Lillian,
Yvonne and Dolores

Frank Simms

Simms with the Sudan Defence Force. He is sitting third from
the right in the second to back row.

Navigator Lofty Carr, aged 98

Trooper Harry Chard, photographed while a prisoner of war in Italy in 1943

The table mountain, near Marada oasis, Libya, where Simms and Chard were captured

Werner Kost, the German who captured them

Certosa di Padula from which Simms tunnelled in the summer of 1942

Forte di Gavi in which both Medd and Simms were imprisoned at the time of the capitulation of Italy in September 1943

Marcus Binney with Frank Abrami (left) and Frank's son
Mario (right)

it; refused to be paid for it, though I said that we had plenty of money. She admitted that they were impossible to get, said that they broke easily, and brought us out a copper one instead.

Peter was rather worried about the Fascist gang till it got dark.

The husband was a jolly little man who had been a prisoner in the last war in Germany. His happiest memories seemed to be of a British transit camp at Verdun where he had stayed some time before being repatriated. He remembered, with the greatest delight, endless bully stew, cigarettes and cinema shows, all free.

I showed him my shoes and he promised to mend them after dinner, and did so, even taking a piece of leather from an old pair of shoes of his own.

For supper we had minestrone, and as a treat some fried toadstools; they weren't very good. They called them Pinetta. They were a yellow-brown colour on top, and spongy yellow underneath. We had plenty of new wine, a sweet, cloudy, refreshing drink. Later, a young man came in, obviously the sweetheart of one of the two good-looking daughters.

We asked about maps and he told us there was a shop that sold maps down the road. 'Maps of Italy—big maps?' we asked incredulously. 'Oh yes.' 'Maps of provinces? Maps of Umbria?' 'Oh, certainly.' He told us Umbria was full of Fascists and we were prepared to believe him.

We slept in the barn that night—our first day in Umbria. We had been free a month.

### Thirty-second Day

WE WENT one and a half miles out of our way to the map-shop, which only had a few maps cut out of newspapers, but where we heard that Italy had declared war on Germany. The whole day was spent going up and down wooded hills and we stayed the night in a well-to-do household, which for mean and grudging kindness was the worst we met, yet it was a big house, with some modern farm machinery. At dinner they said: 'Non c'e vino', in that hard voice which means they have lots but don't intend giving it away.

### Thirty-third Day

THAT night it froze for the first time. We were rather against giving our names so that they should get the promised reward from the Government, but to our surprise, as we left, they gave us a whole loaf to take with us, so we wrote down the usual two lines giving our names and numbers.

We took a long way round to avoid the village of Pietra, reported to be full of Fascists, who had gangs out in the woods looking for prisoners. It was variously reported that an English girl was living there and that three officers had been betrayed recently. We went up a long series of hills and finally came to a little shop that sold (once upon a time) salt and tobacco. We asked the way there and were given some wine and some very good apples. While we were eating these, a party of well-dressed walkers appeared over the pass, and on seeing us exclaimed: 'Two more from the woods!' Well-dressed people unnerved us, as we suspected them of being Fascist, so we started immediately.

Afterwards it struck us that perhaps we had been premature, as they might have been Italian officers in hiding and could have supplied us with maps.

The country was magnificent—great whale-backed downs, and beyond, the highest peaks of the range. There were a lot of horses round about and people seemed to ride them in preference to mules. Our bad map was often a handicap, and once more we found ourselves on the wrong side of a gorge. We were now getting fairly close to Gubbio, though we were never to see it.

About four o'clock, as we came down towards the road, we heard shooting, M.G., mortar, revolver fire, almost like a battle. It grew louder as we went lower, and although we could see nothing when we crossed the road we were still nervous;

somewhere within a few hundred yards were armed men. We started up a track and saw two girls' bicycles leaning against the fence; then we saw coming towards us three young men. We scrambled through the fence and up the hill, which was extremely steep, in record time. It was about the only place we passed where a real effort had been made to prevent erosion; it was terraced by little walls behind which pine trees were planted in rows, and the whole was surrounded by a strong anti-grazing fence. This green and wooded slope was a big contrast to the opposite side of the road which was just bare pink rock, devoid of all vegetation. When we reached the top, we looked down in the direction of the shooting and saw men practising by the side of the road. Obviously, we thought, Fascists. Later we were told that they were probably a partisan band.

On coming down to a very small hamlet, we thought of spending the night there. An old man offered to put us up as long as we liked, but we said we thought it would be better to get a bit nearer to the front, perhaps the Gran Sasso, before lying up and waiting for the Germans to withdraw.

We slept in a double bed. The ceiling of the room was covered with chairs hanging up! I suppose they must have manufactured them on the premises. The floor was covered in saddlery, chaff, apples, garlic and tomatoes.

Peter's boils had been getting steadily worse, and he was once more in considerable pain. I felt he would soon resemble a lunar landscape rather than a human form. However, he remembered that a doctor had told him that garlic was good for them, so he ate two kernels a day, for a few days, and they all practically disappeared.

### Thirty-fourth Day

OUR HOST gave us a lot of wine, and a form of hot bread with a very hard crust, good to eat though highly indigestible. When we finally left the house about ten-twenty, we were rather drunk.

We usually left about six in the morning if we got no breakfast, and about seven to eight if we did.

We soon left the hills and came out on a plain, not such a dangerous plain as the last one, the soil being extremely poor and stony and only in a poor, land-hungry country like Italy, would anyone have attempted to cultivate it.

We were fortunate in finding a track that led us parallel to the road in the right direction for some miles, without a halt.

We crossed the road without difficulty and started to climb some barren and eroded hills. They were of a considerable height and it started to rain. We were now in the mountains where a band of twenty-five thousand armed Italians were living, though neither we nor the local people ever saw them. But from now on, as we approached each great mountain group, the Sibillini, the Gran Sasso, the Maielle, the same number was always reported, when the group was still some way off. We had a long descent in the rain, down a track in a very thick beech forest, and it was getting dark when we finally found a cottage. Their hay was out of doors, and they took us down to another cottage. Here we were able to get the promise of a sleep in the stall, and were allowed to put on our dry clothes in the son's bedroom. He was an escaped soldier. Almost every family had one son escaped and one son missing, a prisoner. The Italians certainly paid a high price for the Roman idea. There was a very motherly woman in the cottage, who gave us a very delicious minestrone made with beans, cabbage and herbs, not the usual one with plain pasta, or one lightly flavoured with tomato and cheese, as in the richer houses. The old father had been a miner in Ohio once and was lame as the result of an accident there.

We slept on the straw in the cattle shed, which was rather cold and very noisy. Domestic animals relieve themselves an enormous number of times during the night.

### *Thirty-fifth Day*

AFTER we had eaten some fried potatoes and bread, we started off down the hill and struck a track running through a very remote valley. We crossed into Marche from Umbria. A boy with a pack mule offered to carry our bundles for us till the next village, and told us how three British officers had been betrayed by a forest guard the week before. He left us in a village where, being Sunday, all were out in their best clothes, and we were offered cigarettes which were always very scarce. We took them.

Our hopes of a big Sunday lunch were dashed, as all we got was bread, grapes and cheese.

We climbed up a very high hill on to a beautiful grassy plateau where we had a glorious view over a flat plain ringed by hills on the west, and the high peaks of the central Apennines on south and east. We saw our first lambs in the afternoon—it seemed very early for them. On our way down the hill we met a couple who had been out shooting. They pointed out our route for the morning, all mountains, and showed us a village in the valley where we would be safe. It was a little bigger than we cared for. They would have put us up themselves, and they had a wireless, but their house was on the main road and they considered it too risky; so did we.

We went down towards the village and met a man who had been picking some very late grapes. He gave us some but they were far too bitter to eat, and we threw them away as soon as he had gone.

We waited above the village till the people came out of church, then made our way to the priest's house. It had started to rain. He had, unfortunately, gone to have a drink in the inn, so we returned to the village and stopped in the first house. This was the post office, and although it was only just six o'clock we got some gnocchi and a few walnuts and bread. There was a doll there—the only child's toy I saw on the journey. We were told we could go the first two kilometres in an ox-cart the next

133

morning, but when we found that it left at half-past three we decided against it. We spent the night in a straw-filled barn in the village, after the usual warnings against smoking had been made to us. An easy day.

### Thirty-sixth Day

WE LEFT as soon as it was light, crossed the road and walked a long way amongst a jumble of wooded mountains, where we could not keep our direction well. The villages we passed through were all full of Montenegrin soldiers. There had been a camp of them close by here, from which they had been released when the armistice was signed. They were not particularly keen on moving, as they got fed by the locals. Their presence, though, meant that the peasants would be less willing to feed us, but we were given bread and wine by an old woman whose Balkan lodgers were painting her bedroom for her. Her own son was missing in Yugoslavia, so she had no news whether he was fighting the Germans or was a prisoner.

We went down a steep mountain path and through to Montecavallo, quite a large village reputed to be Fascist, and then up a wadi whose barren, boulder-strewn bed and rocky eroded sides might have been anywhere in the Red Sea hills.

After we had followed it to its source we climbed a very steep hill, on the top of which was once more open downland. Outside a village we met a young, rather dapper ex-soldier ploughing. He advised us not to stop in the village. However, we did so, and when I returned from washing my socks at the communal fountain I found Peter in the kitchen of a house, so I sat by the fire till he had finished shaving and the son of the house came in, the same soldier who had advised us not to stop there. He seemed surprised to see us.

It was the weekly baking day, and his wife and his sister spent their time feeding the furnace in the next room with bundles of brushwood at the end of long poles. It was hard and hot work and they were both streaming with sweat. The sister had been apprenticed to a dressmaker in Rome, but had run away because she was frightened by the sirens. This was before the city was bombed. Meanwhile, the mother was busy stirring the polenta in the cauldron over the fire in the kitchen. We ate ours out of plates garnished with mushrooms, while the family ate theirs at another table off a communal board.

After dinner the son took us over to hear the news in the village school. No one paid much attention to us, and we heard both the German and English news in Italian.

In between the bulletins we copied the large-scale map of the province in the schoolroom. These always hung there, but unfortunately we had only discovered this two days before. These rooms wore a lopsided look now that only the king's portrait hung there, the Duce's having been destroyed.

We slept the night in a barn belonging to a neighbour.

### *Thirty-seventh Day*

AFTER a breakfast of hot fresh bread (our diet consisted almost entirely of flour in some form or another, and potatoes) we left. The trees were now in their full autumnal colours, and with the flowering leaves of the maples, made the countryside very beautiful.

We crossed a road and climbed a hill and followed a path towards a large village on a hill, which we skirted. We came to another road running south, and beside it a dark, swift stream. We were fortunate enough here to find, on the far side, a very good track which ran parallel to the road, on which we could make good going. We had a shock once, on passing a sentry-box by a weir, but there was nobody in it.

This track led us past a village against which we had been warned, and then over the road, which started to climb through a pass; on our left was the mass of Mount Sibillini. Suddenly we saw a lorry coming over the hill towards us, a very ancient lorry full of refugees, and so we lay down in a field.

135

The top of the pass was grassland, with flocks of sheep and many new-born lambs. The shepherds told us that at this time of year they generally had gone down to winter in the plains by Rome. But this year they were so frightened of German requisitions that they intended postponing their departure as long as possible, hoping that the British would arrive before the snow. We heard that in the town of Norcia, below, ten Italian ex-soldiers had recently been betrayed to the Germans. We met a man and a boy who were evacuees from Rome and had had a shop there. They told us that the whole of Mount Sibillini belonged to them. We drank from a trough and they offered us some food in their house, but as this meant going back, we refused. The man advised us to spend the night in Castellucia, only three hours away over the mountain. He seemed very knowledgeable and full of information and told us he had met two British officers the day before, from Piedmont. Ours had been the only camp in Piedmont, but we failed to recognise them from his description, and never heard of them again.

We followed the path he had pointed out and about forty minutes later came to a farm where we decided to get some food. Peter knocked on the door and a sour-faced woman came out and said: 'Two more refugees,' in a loud voice. Her husband appeared and asked if we were English. He then said that they disapproved of helping prisoners on principle, but since the British Government had promised a reward, they were now prepared to do so. We were kept sitting in the yard while a plate of cold cabbage, with two forks, was prepared, and were then taken into the dark and fly-infested kitchen. No sooner were we inside than one of the daughters appeared with a pencil and paper for us to write down our names, and stood immediately behind my chair, like a waitress in a cheap café.

Suddenly there was an alarm, not of Germans, but from two Italian ex-soldiers returning home. The doors and windows were shut at once, and everyone cowered in the dark and made no answer to their knocking. Italians, after all, had no Government that could offer rewards for hospitality. When I signed the chit, I carefully put one lunch only. Generally we did not leave our names for lunch, but only for supper and lodging, and did not state what we had received.

We carried on down the hill to a monastery which had been abandoned by monks some years ago and was now occupied by a myopic girl and her brother. He had been a prisoner in Australia, of which he had happy memories, and had been repatriated as a medical orderly. I could not help feeling that after this, when his country was so stricken, he might have gone out to help the wounded. Terni, a place which we were bombing a lot then, was only a few miles off, and a passenger train had been badly machine-gunned from the air.

We started the long, long climb towards Castellucia, which lies in the heart of the Sibillini. Below us was Norcia and we continuously crossed the zigzag road from the coast. We met a boy with a donkey, its two low-hanging panniers full of newborn lambs going to spend the winter by the fireside. Castellucia, the boy told us, was an 'oretta'. We climbed and climbed and at last reached the summit. Here we met a party of Italian officers in plain clothes; one of them wore a hairnet. They spent the day in the mountains and returned home after dark. They were frightened of the Germans in Norcia, of whom I suppose there were about six. They advised us to carry sticks to drive off wolves: 'They will be very dangerous soon in the Gran Sasso.'

We came down into the wide grassy plain, ringed with mountains, at the far end of which was the village. We asked some shepherds about lodging; they offered us food and an empty windowless hut for the night. We decided to push on to the village, still an oretta away, before the light went altogether.

Castellucia was a queer town; every house had a yard, a cellar, or a barn full of bleating sheep being locked up for the night. Except for the track we had climbed, and the telephone and electric light, it had no connection with the outer world. In winter, apparently, some people came there to ski. We found our way up its dark and narrow streets, slipping in the mire, to the priest's house, catching a sudden glimpse of magnificence, gold and light, from the open church door. As the priest was at church we were advised to go to the dopolavoro. Whither we were guided by a boy, to find it crowded. Six British soldiers in battledress were listening to the wireless. We bought them some wine and had enough cigarettes left for one apiece. They told us that they had no money and had been forced to offer their pullovers in exchange for supper. Peter arranged to get them back and I gave them two hundred lire, which pleased them. We were then given a message to go and see the priest, so we said goodbye to the soldiers and went to the priest's house where we had supper of minestrone, bread, cheese and wine. We were surprised that the priests should be so anti-German; they were prepared for any reprisals against them after the war. They were not very anti-Russian; they thought they had changed their politics completely as a result of the war. Finland, the real martyr of the war, was the country for whom they felt most sorry. After supper we went back to the dopolavoro and found two more British officers there; we all had a drink together. The troops seemed to be celebrating their increase in wealth by getting drunk, so we went to our beds, a barn above a sheep stall, full of straw and very warm. We slept very well there. That night there was two hundred pounds in rewards going for anyone who had dared to capture the lot of us.

### Thirty-eighth Day

IN THE village shop we had a warming breakfast of four biscuits made of figs and flour and two glasses of Marsala with egg. The village stood on a little hill and the plain, covered as it was in mist, would have been impossible to cross without a compass had we not had a line of telephone wires to follow.

It was good to walk on the flat for a change. After about five miles we started to go down, passing a ski-ing hut.

We crossed the road from Norcia and were now below the mist. We went down a very steep and broken slope on which Peter, as usual, got a long way ahead. We skirted a village called Capo d' Acqua, which we regarded as too large to be safe. Later we learnt there were seventeen British prisoners living there. We heard strong rumours once more of armed bands, this time reinforced by parachutists.

We came into Lazio, in the same province as Rome and beyond which was the Abruzzi. We crossed the main road between Amatrice and the sea, under a culvert, waded across a stream and followed a path at the foot of the range. On top, we were told, were three German observation posts.

About three o'clock we passed a shock-headed Yugo-Slav (he looked like Struwelpeter), with a smart middle-aged woman, who asked us if we wanted food. We asked for some fruit—they were eating pears—but we didn't get any.

We came to a village and asked for water. A fat, motherly woman in a dirty apron came to the door—it was a big house—and asked us in. She cooked a minestrone specially for us, and fried some meat, and then suggested that we spend the night there. Peter's boots needed mending, and she thought the cobbler might be back in the evening. It was always nice to be asked to stop, instead of begging to do so; Peter had to do the asking, his Italian being far better than mine. His boots were flat-heeled and he was beginning to find this tiring, so he had made an imitation arch by filling his sock with chaff.

Having decided to stop, we went down to the village fountain with all our dirty clothes, and by a judicious amount of sighing and fumbling, I soon persuaded an old woman to wash them for us. We carried her copper water jar back to her house, and she asked us in for breakfast the next morning.

Our hostess had six sons, and five of them were at home, all exceedingly tall and well-made. The youngest was missing in Greece. They were a well-off household and even had a wireless set, though the current wasn't strong enough for us to hear it.

One of the women of the house had an unhealthy-looking baby, aged about six months, which was always being given great smacking kisses on the mouth by any of the huge sons who was near it. It never showed any pleasure at being kissed, rather it tended to cry as it saw one of them approaching it with a tender look in his eye. I felt rather sorry for it. The kitchen, as usual, was a mass of flies.

There was polenta for supper and the table was covered with a piece of board about the size of a door; the huge cauldron was then tilted until the viscous dough had covered it to about half-inch thickness. Everyone except the women, including the mother, stood up and started in with forks as soon as the polenta had been garnished with bits of meat and mushrooms, thrown on it as by a man sowing the seed. We weren't offered any at first, an old crone remarking that we had had minestrone. However, the mother, who had now succeeded by luck in getting a seat, said we could have some, and we were given forks, and we, too, began, although more slowly, to carve out crescents and bays and eat our way towards the middle.

Afterwards an old beggar woman came in and cleaned off the bits; she complained there was not much left, and the old crone again pointed us out.

We were told if we stayed up till ten o'clock the current would be strong enough for us to hear the news. But at about eight-thirty a large party of young men came in, and after a few minutes we were asked if we wouldn't like to go to bed. It became so pointed that we were forced to agree, and were packed off to a hay-barn. The shock-headed Yugo-Slav was in the party and much later, after midnight, he came in and slept beside us.

Peter had not got his boots repaired.

## Thirty-ninth Day

WE TOLD Signora Budini, the hostess, that we had been asked out to breakfast, but she insisted on our having coffee and milk and bread with the family. Her husband, a rather distinguished-looking man, told us that we might be in the Gran Sasso within three or four days. (We reached it that night.) As soon as we could, we left and went down for our second breakfast. Our new hostess offered us chairs and went off to the fountain to get some water. She must have heard there that we had already breakfasted, as she said: 'But you have had coffee and milk.' She gave us, therefore, bread, wine and ewe's milk cheese, very white and hard, and without much taste; as well as a bunch of grapes each—they were hanging from the ceiling, the last grapes of any kind we were given, till some were handed in through the bus window between Foggia and Bari. She gave us a generous piece of bread and cheese for lunch.

We started off about eight-thirty a.m. and were advised to keep in the chestnut woods between the mountains and the open fields. Two miles to our right was Amatrice, a big town which had been visited the day before by Germans and Fascists rounding up workmen for forced labour.

The woods were full of people picking chestnuts, and the hills echoed with the sound of cowbells and the raucous cries of shepherds. We climbed up a long grassy ridge, past grazing sheep and lambs, and emerged on a plateau definitely in the Abruzzi.

Ahead of us we could see a lake, and as it was a warm day, we thought of bathing. It was the first lake we had seen since the day we had left Roggio. Later, we thought we would be rather foolish to bathe in an open piece of water, and as we were following a reasonable-sized stream, we stopped instead at a pool below a small waterfall. After we had eaten our bread and cheese, we went on. Ahead of us were the great peaks of the Gran Sasso, and on our right a small hill-town perched above the lake, called Campobasta. The lake was quite new, the result

141

of flooding part of the plateau, and was alive with moorhens. Its shallow water was intensely blue, and it was about fifteen miles round. It was very beautiful, but largely spoilt by a road that was carried across it by an ugly trestle bridge. The main road ran along the lakeside, and as everyone assured us that there were neither Germans nor Fascists about, we followed it to find it crowded with people, principally women with donkeys laden with firewood. Their curiosity was intense. Every one in turn asked us where we were going and where we came from; it became rather aggravating. They were very different from the placid cultivators in the plain north of Florence, who had paid no attention to our sudden incursion into their vineyards.

When we came to the end of the lake, we met two charcoal burners with donkeys, and asked them where we could halt for the night. Ahead of us apparently, and much to our surprise, was the main Rome-Termoli road, which was used a lot by Germans, and the village on it had a pull-in for their drivers: so they advised us not to stop there. They took us to a very poor cottage, but the woman refused us and we had not the heart to press her. They then advised us to walk to a workers' camp where some blasting operations in connection with the lake hydraulic scheme were going on. We followed their directions and came to a series of quarries connected by trolley-lines and cables, where there were about fifty men at work. The foreman refused to put us up, as it was too dangerous, but the workmen had a whip-round and gave us various scraps of bread which they had saved from their lunches. One of them was evidently so ashamed of the size of his offering that he wrapped it up. It was a disappointment to us later when we opened it, as we had expected to find bacon. The foreman pointed out a valley the other side of the road, leading into the Gran Sasso, where, he said, was a cabin inhabited by three Englishmen. He also told us that on our way to it we would pass the engineers' mess where one of their wives would cook us some minestrone. We went down a very steep hill towards the road. The engineers' mess was beside it, and our path led directly behind it. Sitting in an upstairs sitting-room—and how well-furnished and comfortable it looked—were two women. We thought the house was too dangerous to stop in, and went on across the road, where an enormous dam was being built in the gorge. When we regained the shelter of the woods I turned and waved to them. It must have been quite interesting to live, as they did, on a main fugitive route and watch the stream go past. In the wood we met a shepherd returning his flock to fold, in the setting sun. He showed us the way to the house of a forest guard. However, the latter refused to put us up and showed us the path to a refuge in the woods at the foot of the mountains, about three miles off; he said he was already suspected by the Germans of helping prisoners. Rather foolishly we failed to ask for anything to eat. He was quite a friendly old man and told us the way over the Sasso that we should follow in the morning.

We walked quickly through the darkening woods; a stream ran beside the path which, for once, neither petered out nor divided. We reached the shelter as the last light failed. There were three buildings—one had a big white plaster façade and was an abandoned ruin, the other two were locked.

We broke down the doors by hurling lumps of marble at the locks, which Peter tried to open with wire. At last we smashed open one door and found we were in a chapel, which was evidently not abandoned. We went to work on the other door and ultimately broke it open, to find ourselves in a huge barn with about fifty bales of compressed hay in a corner. We soon got a fire going.

From the ceiling of the barn a badger's skin stretched on a frame was hanging. We put the door back as best we could to cover the doorway—it was very cold—and then moved the bales of hay as close to the fire as we dared. We made ourselves a beautiful bed out of them and were very comfortable. Before turning in, we went down over the wet grass to the stream, whose icy waters flowed too fast to reflect the stars. We each had left a crust of bread for breakfast in the morning.

### Fortieth Day

AFTER eating a bit of stale bread and repairing some of the damage we had done to the doors of the chapel and the barn we started off; it was very cold until the sun cleared the mountains. After a while the track narrowed and divided; we passed several complicated stone-walled sheepfolds, the trees ended, and we began to climb the Gran Sasso.

The great white marble peaks of the group were in front of us as we passed to the right of Monte Corno. When the track split once more we paused to discuss the route. In front of us were the clustered peaks which the Forest Guard the night before had told us to leave on our left. The track through seemed to peter out altogether; on the other side of the group was quite a well-defined track and up it we toiled for about half an hour, to find ourselves confronted by a wild vista of mountains and ravines, of white rock and sparse brown grass. We knew then that we had come wrong and tried to find a way round to the other path. There was nothing but a precipice and we were forced to retrace our steps and then climb up as the Forest Warden had advised us. The only thing that cheered me was the sight of the lake we had passed the day before, catching the sunrise and slowly becoming more and more intensely blue as the sun rose in the sky.

We crossed the pass, now in the clouds, and halted in the sunshine below them. The Gran Sasso was not as wild as we had hoped; below was a cluster of houses and we could see in the valley to the south, some five miles away, a town, and beyond, in the next valley, a city, and that city was Aquila. I really began to feel that we were getting somewhere at last. Aquila was by Sulmona, and Sulmona was almost level with Rome. We were in the same half of Italy as the British now.

As we went down the grassy hillside, smelling of the South Downs, we saw an RAF attack on a convoy near the Aquila road.

At the foot of the hill we met a man with a well-laden mule, who offered us lunch in the fields. He said prisoners were working there and living in the huts we had seen from above. We discovered they were all Slavs and the huts were summer huts for sheep. Lunch, with two Slav soldiers, the old man and his daughter, was a good meal of bread, mashed potatoes flavoured with green peppers still warm in an iron pot, plenty of bread and walnuts and some bacon. To wash it down there was a bottle of wine and a cask of water. We were rather tempted to stop; to be assured of food and lodging near the front was attractive.

While the others went on hoeing potatoes and the old man packed the mule, we lay on a grassy strip between the stony fields and rested in the sun. At about four o'clock we approached the man and asked him about getting our shoes repaired. But he didn't seem very concerned; like so many people in the Abruzzi, he had been very hospitable to begin with and then lost interest. Anyhow, he now was not very keen about our working for him, so we decided to go on, hoping that when we had crossed the Pescara River we would find another farmer who would offer us work till the British arrived. We had no idea as to how we would ever cross the German line, and sometimes imagined we would be forced to retreat as they did, slowly to the north, conforming to their movements.

The only place to get our shoes done seemed to be Assergi, the town on our left. But was it safe? The old man said it was full of Fascists and Germans. We were both rather worried but, as usual, the Lord provided.

We were hanging around waiting for it to get darker, when we saw a woodcutter and his wife in a field. He also told us the town was very Fascist, and upon sighting a group of men, including a Forest Guard, reputed to be a spy, urged us to meet them further on. We waited by the stream until they came in sight with their donkey. They gave us some bread and told us to go down a track to the right where there was a mill that had recently put up three escaped prisoners.

We reached it in the dark, to be told that the owner was away, so we sat down with two old women, one of whom was carding wool, for a long time.

A rather dour-looking woman with a weather-beaten face took us home, right into the centre of the town, a little house of three rooms. We sat down by the fire and the neighbours and her mother-in-law bustled in, one with wood, one with pasta, another with bacon and another with wine. In the room was a Madonna in a wooden folding frame. She made a circuit through the town and stopped one night in every house. I was pleased to think that our stay should coincide with hers. One of the party was a boy of eleven. It was a striking example of the dominance of the male that only we and this boy drank any of the two bottles of wine that were provided, although the mother-in-law, aged seventy, who lived opposite, had walked five miles each way to till some barren field that day. We had a very good minestrone, our hostess continually ejaculating: 'Eat! Eat!' as she gave us another helping. She produced an enormous loaf—we only saw half of it—but it was originally a 10 kilo or 25lb. loaf, all home-made.

Her husband was a prisoner in South Africa, and she had not seen him for six years.

We expected to leave early, and after dinner we were taken upstairs to a room with a double bed, which almost filled it. Peter, trying to be polite and appreciative, said: 'I hope we are not turning anyone out of his bed.' Our hostess, Signora Mosca, pulled back the coverlet and, showing us the spotless sheets, said: 'No, they're perfectly clean.'

In our haversack we still had bread and potatoes and walnuts that the peasant had given us at lunch.

### Forty-first Day

WHEN we woke up the next morning it was light. Kind and brave Mrs Mosca had not bothered about the risk of our staying the day in the house. After coffee, and bread to dip in it, she took our boots off to the cobbler and we were locked in the house. On the wall, there was a fearful Fascist calendar of gaudy victories in Ethiopia and Spain, which her husband had sent her, and a few postcards stuck in the mirror-frame, lovers' postcards, a view of Florence and a Carabiniero on horseback jumping through flames. These were in the parlour, a little room off the kitchen where we had eaten the night before. It was a safer room, as it didn't open straight on to the street. In one corner the wall had recently been plastered, and behind it was their reserve stock of flour, hidden from the Germans.

When she came back, she brought us a guide-book of Central Italy with a map which Peter copied out—all the country between Aquila and the Sangro, where we then thought the front was.

After a lunch of gnocchi, cheese, bacon, bread and new wine, with an enormous quantity of walnuts, which, being men, we ate alone, we went to bed for the afternoon. When we woke we had some supper. While we were eating and our hostess was saying: 'Eat!' and cutting huge hunks of bread continuously, a man came in, an officer, though not a regular, and whose wife was the schoolmistress. He suggested that we should go to his house and hear the wireless, and asked us what we wanted. We suggested maps and a knife, and they all then argued as to who should give us food for our journey. Our hostess seemed to think it was a reflection on her hospitality if she did not supply it. She had brought our shoes back. The patches on mine now covered nearly all the sole, and she gave us a new pair of homespun, home-knitted socks. We went to hear the wireless in the officer's house where his wife, two South Africans and his sister were. The prisoners came in to feed each evening, and spent the day in a cave. They said they told everyone to move on, but they seemed to be pleased to stop themselves. There was the usual confusion of the wavelength, so that we missed the first English and Italian broadcasts of the BBC, and finally heard Radio Algiers. The Italians seemed quite incapable of getting any station twice. While we were waiting our hostess produced some tea. This had come from the Red Cross and had been given to her by some prisoners whom she had helped earlier on.

When we did hear the news, it wasn't very good; the front was still static somewhere beyond the Sangro—no landing in the Adriatic—Isernia still untaken. Come on, Montgomery! But they admitted he knew more about strategy than they did. We got back to the house rather late and felt rather guilty about keeping Mrs Mosca up. She told us that three Germans had asked the way to the mill that evening. We hoped only to requisition food.

She and the officer then produced the food for us—three loaves of bread, bacon, cheese, apples and nuts. We had to be given a spare pillow-case in which to carry it all! Once more we went to bed.

Although the Madonna had left the house, I hoped she would continue to bless this poor, lonely and good woman.

### Forty-second Day

WE HAD an alarm clock and Mrs Mosca to wake us (we always referred to her like that, she was too good to seem foreign), and at four-forty-five we were drinking coffee. Then, with our bags full of food, and our hearts full of gratitude, she led us through the still sleeping town. She started us on the path into the hills, and we said goodbye. As we went higher, it got colder, and we were walking over frozen grass, with our hands quite numb. There was a wonderful sunrise that morning, and we could see all the peaks of the Gran Sasso and the Maielle and the ridges beyond Sulmona catching the light in turn. On our left we could see the Bosco Imperatore, a national park, and the funicular and the hotel where Mussolini had been imprisoned. There were still many Germans living up there.

For once, having climbed, we were not faced by an immediate descent, and instead walked along a grassy plateau. There were many refugees about, driving their cattle and sheep up to the mountains for safety. But when the winter came they would have to go down. In some places long slits were driven into the rock where the cattle slept at night, the doors blocked with furze. Very warm places to hide in, we thought.

We ate for breakfast the remains of the potatoes, bread and bacon which the peasant had given us for lunch two days before.

Then followed a beautiful walk along a series of grassy ridges. We met an old man on a pony who had been a miner in Pennsylvania: he gave us three apples.

We passed Castelmonte, a remote mountain town, served surprisingly by three main roads and used by the Germans for their wounded.

Near a road a man started calling to us in English when we were still about four hundred yards away. This was always rather disconcerting. For lunch we stopped at a well, by an isolated farm, and were eating bread and bacon, when the farmer sent his daughter out with cheese for us. It was a very warm day and we drank a lot from the well bucket. To cross the Pescara River where we intended, which was about twenty miles east of Sulmona, we were advised to take a very steep path up a hill to avoid two very Fascist villages. This really meant one or two Fascists, but we were taking no risks, and decided to make this detour. Everyone we met had been in Pennsylvania—an old shepherd, a string of charcoal-burners coming down with their mules, and then a second, who insisted on giving us a big piece of bread. In a beech-wood, on the top, we found no track going where we wanted. The ridge itself ran the wrong way and clouds were coming down in the valley below us. Dejectedly we made our way to a distant grass-covered peak with a white wooden beacon on the top. But we could see nothing from there; the distant peaks of the Maielle across the river and those by Sulmona stood above the clouds. We were on the eastern side of the Apennines, but fortunately could not see the sea owing to the clouds. I had a feeling that as long as Peter, being a sailor, didn't see it, we were all right.

We had some bread on the top and Peter nearly left our new penknife behind. We could see nothing in the way of houses, and it was already getting cold and the sun was low. We went down a very steep, grassy slope on the west side, then changed over to a grassy track on the other side of the crest, and here in a beech wood we found a path, a big, well-kept path, down which we went very fast, for we had both night and fog to contend with. We met no one but a sheepdog, which, soured by our old clothes, came and barked at us.

As it was getting dark we came to a road and met a man who told us there were houses close by, and when we heard noises of people we should turn off the track. It was lucky we met him as we would never have seen these houses in the dark and fog.

When we reached the village, which was very small, we asked a woman if she knew where we could stop, and she said: 'Nowhere—the Germans come here often.' This was a blow and we were still arguing when someone plucked at my sleeve and said: 'Come in here.' We went in and found another miner from Pennsylvania, and were immediately given a plate of gnocchi and two forks between us—the family had been at supper. We were both very thirsty and water was produced in a smart blue glass water-jug. When I asked for glasses I was informed that everyone drank out of the jug. The family were very much against our trying to cross the Pescara valley. It was far too dangerous—pickets and cycle patrols everywhere—

seventeen British prisoners had been caught crossing in the last two days—six had been shot; we would do better to go into the mountains where there was a village full of armed British parachutists. They were not interested in our story, which was a relief. They had seen too many prisoners for that. We spent the night in a barn with thatched sides, but they lent us plenty of blankets.

### Forty-third Day

WE HAD promised to be away early, but could not find the cord which the Borsellis had given us by Borgo San Lorenzo and had to tie our blanket up with string and bootlaces.

We met a lot of people and they were all very gloomy. 'You will never cross the valley,' they said; 'you ought to find a house to stay in till the British come—it is madness to try.'

Except, perhaps, for the Genoa-Milan road, this Rome-Pescara road was the worst we had to cross.

It consisted of a railway, a river reputed to be unfordable and a main road, much used and closely patrolled by the Germans. Nearer to Sulmona, all three ran through a gorge—later, till they reached the coastal plain, they remained fairly close. The coastal plain was too dangerous. Peter had once been in a prison at Sulmona. To the west of the town we could cross them separately, for they all divided, and this would bring us back into the main mountain chain, where, presumably, the fighting was least heavy. This last supposition proved to be totally wrong. While we had breakfast in a bamboo thicket by a stream, we decided to go to the west of Sulmona. It meant losing a day and we admitted we were scared, but it was better to be cautious.

Following our new direction, we kept in the hills parallel to the dreaded valley, passing an ancient Italian sitting naked in the sun. Then we met a boy who said it was possible to cross, that three officers had stayed in their house the night before and were even now attempting the crossing. He was a sensible boy. He pointed us out the direction, which was by the mouth of the gorge where all three, road, railway and river, emerged. We decided to go down and have a look at the valley—it did not commit us, after all. We went down, crossing over a road, and picking tomatoes from a garden, to a place where from the edge of a wood we could overlook the valley and observe movement on the road. Just as we paused a man told us that there were no German pickets on the road, but that some of the houses below us had Germans billeted in them. We ate our lunch of bread and bacon and watched. The railway seemed unguarded and unused; the river some way beyond it looked swift and deep; but at some places it was at least out of sight of both the railway and the road.

The road seemed to be unguarded except for two leisurely cyclists, perhaps policemen; there was a great deal of traffic on it, but beneath it there were culverts with ditches, along which we could crawl. I was for going on. Peter was for waiting till dark, but I persuaded him to go and ask which houses were occupied by Germans, and we learnt that none of those ahead were. Then, to our left, we heard a burst of Tommy-gun fire. Testing it out? Shooting at a fugitive? We never knew. I led the way down through the vineyards, and after a bit stopped at a house for advice. An elderly woman said we could never cross the Pescara on foot—it was far too deep and swift, and she would show us a safe way over.

She must have had a natural bent for fieldcraft; we never mistook her hand signals. We were on a different track from hers; she led us to a railway bridge, and over the river—beyond it was the road, so we were at the very mouth of the gorge. We waited behind a bamboo thicket till the road was clear and then started across; suddenly she called to us to lie down as two German lorries rumbled past, then we were across the road, up the other side, giving a quick wave back to the sporting 'old woman' striding along on her bare feet. We had crossed the Pescara valley, and it was the sixth week today. We knew the next river was the Sangro, and we could hear gunfire.

We went up the hill and came to a house where the owner, who had also been to America, suggested we should stay the night. We could reach no more houses that night, he said, and we were safe there. We agreed, though we had never stopped so close to a main road before, and it was only two o'clock. It was, too, a day to celebrate. He sent us out a plate of hot minestrone and some bread, and then from a village in the valley a woman appeared with a basket, for her husband, a soldier who was hiding nearby. He gave us a big plate of cold macaroni between us, and a chop each, and some wine. We sat above the road and watched the traffic. A party of young Italians who were in hiding came and sat with us. They told us that all the ambulances on the road below us were full of their pork, that a company of the Fascist M. Battalion, Mussolini's own, had arrived and was going to comb the hills for fugitives, both English and Italian. They were billeted now at Tocco, a town a few miles to the East.

Suddenly the alarm went—the Germans were coming, and we all had to flee up the steep precipitous face of the gorge. Halfway up, Peter and I stopped with one Italian soldier in a sheltered position, a perfect machine-gun post dominating the road, and almost unassailable. I pointed this out. 'We would use it,' said the soldier, 'but they might bomb it.' Peter pointed out that a ledge halfway up a precipitous cliff was almost impossible to hit. He still said it was too dangerous.

When the all-clear went we all scrambled back again. There had never been any Germans at all. However, four British soldiers had arrived. They had been in a working camp at Aquila and had been free since the armistice. They, too, had been to the mill at Assergi. We were not very pleased to see them, thinking of our long walk from Piedmont. We sat round a fire indoors afterwards, though we had no supper. Our host's mother was there, aged eighty-three. They came out to this house in the summer and she worked in the fields. She had seen a lot of changes in her life, but she still knew that old women in Italy must earn their keep.

After the Pescara river, we began to live more roughly. The nights of beds and hot suppers off plates were over, though we didn't know it yet.

### Forty-fourth Day

THE ITALIAN soldiers guided us over the mountain. They spent the day there and their women carried on in their absence, did all their own work plus the men's, and then cooked food and carried it four or five miles into the mountains each day. They, too, of course, had to face the German foraging patrols or the Fascist Militia if they came. Two Cypriots had also spent the night at that house. We all split up, and Peter and I walked on the west side of the valley—beyond it was a road with villages running towards the Sangro, at the foot of the main Maielle group. It was a dreary day. I had piles and Peter had such violent pains in his stomach that he had to lie down occasionally. For breakfast we were given bread spread with meat or green peppers by some more Italian soldiers. The going was awful, all loose stones, and our host had disturbed us by saying: 'In two more days you will be through.' At least we had learnt there wasn't a continual line of trenches and barbed-wire across the country, but presumably everything was guarded by machine-gun fire.

We ate our lunch, while some children offered us bread, and we watched a family of peasants bringing down tree trunks on the end of a wire, sliding down specially made paths. We passed a man chipping logs who refused to tell Peter the way, and did not return my 'good day'. Later it got misty, so we came down off the endless ridges of stones, and met a shepherd who pointed out some German armoured cars in the valley, off the road, which alarmed us. All the woods were full of Italian soldiers in hiding. We were looking for a shepherd's hut, and finally we saw one, a few yards above a stretch of road which had been under construction and was now abandoned. In the hut was a Montenegrin and nearby a cave with a little straw on the floor where Peter went to lie down. The Slav had some potatoes but no bread, so I gave him some and we boiled some of his potatoes. He could speak little Italian; he was a partisan and only recently a prisoner. He said it was impossible to cross the Sangro or the road in front of it, as there were German machine-gun posts all the way. He had spent five days trying to get through, and the Germans were always testing out their fixed lines. None of the peasants forward would give him food. He advised us to stop where we were and get someone to feed us. He had found a woman who brought him the potatoes and had given him ten lire. Finding this was all he had, I gave him fifty more and produced some walnuts, which he cracked in his teeth. He didn't mind our sleeping in the cave, as he only used it in the daytime; at night he sat over the fire in this lean-to straw hut. When the potatoes were boiled, we ate them in our fingers and I filled my hat with some for Peter, who was feeling better. We put on all our clothes, and, wrapped up in our blanket, we were soon asleep; although the cave had a big entrance for its width—it was really a fissure with a top to it—and the mist came in, we both slept well.

### Forty-fifth Day

IT WAS a very foggy morning and we were unable to move off till after eight. The Montenegrin came to say goodbye to us and looked rather wistfully at our spare shirts and trousers and our woollen vests as we packed them in bundles. We walked down the hill the few yards towards the abandoned road. He told us to go in the opposite direction—there were too many German posts the way we were going—but we went on because there was a string of about six mules accompanied by three Italians coming towards us. Peter asked the leading man the way. He seemed a little dumb and the third man pushed his way towards us. He, too, was dressed much like an Italian, but on his head was a drill cap and round his waist a belt with 'Gott mit uns' on the buckle. He drew a heavy revolver from his belt and said aggressively: 'Papier?' Peter pointed out quietly in Italian that the man was a German. He ran his hands over us for arms and then opened our bag and glanced in it. He did not guess we were not Italians. Peter then asked him if we could go, but he signalled to us to fall in behind the mules; he did not return his revolver to his holster but tucked it in his belt. Rather ostentatiously he showed one of his Wop prisoners a grenade he carried in his trouser pocket.

After a few yards he signed to us to put our kit into the mule panniers, which were all full of blankets and bits of carpets that he had taken from the district. We fell in again and moved off. We were still within a hundred yards of the cave where presumably our Montenegrin friend was watching. Feeling I was not being very Italian, I wrung my hands and uttered a loud 'Porca Madonna'. The road now led directly below the cave and then started to climb a hill with a wooded slope on the right leading down to a stream. Visibility, I suppose, was about sixty yards. The German was eating a piece of bread with his right hand. That meant he would probably have to change hands to shoot.

I leapt down the bank; within a few yards what I had hoped was a single bush that I could hurdle proved to be some cut-down beech undergrowth, and I was flat on my face immediately below the road and about twelve feet from the Hun. He had turned on Peter, who seized one of the Italians and held him in front of him. The soldier drew his revolver and turned on me. I was getting up. Peter bolted; and as I got up I saw him fall beside me—there had been a shot—I thought he was hit—I couldn't stop—he would have groaned if he'd been hit—I was running and a bullet pinged the earth about three feet to my right—Peter was level with me—he went to cross the stream and slipped—he was up—we ran on. Suddenly there was a big explosion behind us: the German had thrown the grenade. We ran on and were swallowed up by the mist.

Suppose he had thrown the grenade when I was getting up and Peter falling down! We had given the Montenegrin an exciting five minutes. I do not suppose the whole affair lasted longer than that.

We had nothing to carry—no spare clothes, no blankets, and the remains of our Assergi food had gone; a good thing, we decided. We were not cautious enough. Now we had to get through quickly before the weather broke. Both of us had such faith that we would get through that we had never felt any doubt while we had been with the German.

Part of our new policy was to have as much food as possible. We would ask everyone we saw for food, in case the majority refused us, as the Slav foretold. We immediately picked up a potato each from a field.

It was a difficult day what with the fog, no map showing the country and no compass. We went up and down mountain slopes in the forest and succeeded in getting some bread from some shepherds, after a refusal from some evacuees hiding in the trees.

We did find that the road we had seen below us the day before did not lead anywhere, as it wasn't yet finished. But we were always losing our way, and the fog was turning to rain. My piles were much the same, though Peter's stomach seemed to be cured. Towards midday we scrambled down the mountain, where we heard sounds of a woodcutter; we found two men who invited us to sit under their umbrella while they worked. Their boy had gone to fetch their lunch. 'No more laws,' said the younger one; 'we can cut where we like now,' as he neatly cut down a young tree in two strokes. He said there was another river and road between us and the Sangro. The front was not a fixed one and was somewhere beyond the Sangro. In a village on the road behind us was a German post with an Arab cook— he didn't look so well as he had when they first caught him; he had been a prisoner trying to get through. Their boy came back on a pony, and we had a hot lunch of mashed potatoes and polenta. The rain had stopped and the clouds had lifted, so that the woodcutter could point out a pass over the mountains. As we were moving off with bread in our pockets once more, six Italian ruffians appeared, who had been conscripted for work on the Castel de Sangro position and had deserted.

We started on the way the woodcutter had shown us, but the clouds had come down again and we couldn't see in the wood which path led to the pass. We wasted about an hour before we got another glimpse of it. It was a steep climb, and when we reached the top we could again see nothing. The path was one adapted for pulling down tree trunks, therefore well-banked, but the bushes overhung it, so we got very wet. When near the bottom, we saw a big farmhouse and a village and we could hear traffic on the road. All traffic was *German*. We found a cabin for the night, though it had no door. Peter's boots were again split down the side, and he sat down to mend them by the fading light, while I rushed out to get wood before it rained and was fortunate in finding a lot of sloe boughs which were dry inside. I pulled out a post from a barbed-wire fence and brought it, with about ten feet of wire I couldn't untie, to the hut. Then it poured with rain. This wood, with the help of a few bits we found on the floor and two beams from beneath the corrugated iron roof, kept the fire going all night. We lay down and dried our clothes. Later, when it was my turn to watch the fire, a boy came in looking for a lost cow. He refused to sit by the fire and promised to bring us milk and bread in the morning at five o'clock. He came in several times and said that the road below was not guarded. About midnight we each roasted our potato. By then the night was clear and full of stars. If we didn't sleep much we were at least dry, warm and rested. There was a lot of traffic on the road below, and the river sounded as if it flowed very fast.

### Forty-sixth Day

WE MOVED about four-forty-five and went very cautiously down a very steep and muddy series of ploughed fields. There were no signs of Germans, except for a few lights in neighbouring cottages and a newly dug anti-tank ditch. We got to the road— not such a big one as we had expected; we splashed across an icy-cold, knee-deep river. When dawn came we were walking over grassy ridges. In front of us was a range of mountains, and beyond that was the Sangro. 'One more river, one more river to Jordan.' We came to a large encampment of shepherds, but the headman, who came from Termoli, refused to give us anything to eat. He showed us a path over the ridge where were farms, he said, that would feed anybody. He pointed out that the Germans were taking five thousand sheep and goats from this district alone.

Before we crossed the ridge we met some more shepherds, who, after a while, gave us half a loaf of bread. We then went on towards the generous farms. The woods on the range were full of cattle being hidden, and some fugitive boys gave us six big potatoes, which we kept in reserve. Later we came to the farmhouses, and at each we were refused even maize, though the ceilings of all Italian peasant kitchens are hung thick with the yellow cobs.

After a while we met a man who told us that the Sangro valley was full of Germans and advised us to 'stop at once if challenged, as otherwise they shoot'. He did, however, offer to take us home and give us a meal, but we decided his house was rather out of the way. We went on towards a village perched precariously on top of a rock, and near it we met three women.

They offered us food in their house in the village. We considered this too dangerous also, so they said they would bring it out to us in the wood. About an hour later they returned with two big pieces of bread and a piece of cheese. There was a road below us, and while we ate, their brother, aged about eighteen, gave us a route which ultimately proved quite wrong. Suddenly a German lorry came up the road; we all fled farther into the wood. The girls were sent to reconnoitre and the brother went farther off. Later, the girls came back, giving the usual two-note whistle used by Italians in these circumstances. The Germans could have caught any number of them by going into a forest and giving this whistle. Their brother would not be coming back, but would like our names (presumably for the promised reward). We gladly gave them, and they left.

The route we had been given led us along by some precipitous marble cliffs. Fortunately we met a woodcutter who had been a prisoner in Egypt, and he gave us a route at right angles to the one we were following, crossing the Sangro and going up through a wood over the next range, leaving Capracotta well to the west; then it was only four hours' easy descent to Agnone.

At first we had to keep on crossing a road as we descended. We were approaching a group of houses, when it began to rain, and some peasants ran out to us to beg us to enter their house and were amazed at our refusal. Soon we found a culvert under the railway, with two old women sheltering under it. After a quick look, much to their amazement, we waded straight into the river, which was waist deep and very fast. However, we were already so wet that the water seemed quite warm.

When I was across I looked round and saw Peter hauling himself on to a rock in midstream like a seal. We plunged into a wood which was so thick that it might well be called impenetrable—it would have been to anyone who wasn't a fugitive. It tore our clothes, heavy with water; and Peter's trousers, always thin, were in ribbons in the most unfortunate places. We were, at least, across the Sangro. A road ran across the wood; and approaching it, as we saw a lorry parked there by a tent, we made a detour, crossing near a place where a soldier's washing was hanging up, but we thought he must be away—he wouldn't have let it hang up in the rain. On the other side of the road the wood was almost as bad. I found a German newspaper dated 15th October, under a tree: we pushed on even more quickly. We were now both shivering with cold; but we still had a piece of bread under our coats which we tried in vain to keep dry.

Above us on the crest was another precarious rock village. We climbed on. Surely we would be safe up there. Then, on our left, we saw smoke from a cottage almost hidden in the trees. It was a new house full of women, busy scrubbing pigs' intestines and making sausages; they were from the village above and had had three of their pigs killed by the Germans living there, so they had fled down here and slaughtered the rest, prior to walling up the meat. We sat by the fire which was built into the corner of the wall, but we couldn't dry very adequately by it. Soon we were each given a bowl of cold polenta, and later another bowl full of delicious bits of very fat fried bacon and some bread. The husband of one of them came in, divided his own bacon between us and gave Peter another pair of trousers. These people were wonderful in their spontaneous hospitality, and they were in trouble, too. 'If the British don't come soon, we will have nothing,' the women kept saying. We asked if we could sleep on the floor that night, but were refused. Some of the people who lived there were not relations, but friends, and might not be trusted. It seemed strange to live with people who might betray you. However, the man knew of a cabin nearby, and off we went, having been lent greatcoats, and he took a big shovelful of coals from the fire to light one for us.

The cabin was well-hidden between rocks and trees. It had a fireplace in the middle and bunks full of bracken round it. He lit the fire and we collected some wood; it was still raining. He promised to show us the way before dawn. It was easy to get through the lines, he had heard. We offered him fifty pounds to take us through, but he refused. He was a married man.

There were a few blankets in the cabin but they were damp, as was the wood which smoked. We roasted our six potatoes, one of Peter's a bit battered, as, while we were drying, the children had kicked it around a bit. The people there had told us that we had been very lucky to get across the valley, as it was full of Germans. The rain, perhaps, had kept them under cover.

### Forty-seventh Day

THE FIRE went out as soon as we ceased to tend it, and we spent a rather uncomfortable night. The man from the house arrived before we were up, and brought with him a fair-haired soldier in an Italian air-force uniform. His appearance gave us a terrible shock as we stepped out into the dim light; we thought he was a German officer. They took us a little way and told us the route to follow. It was the first time we were given one that we didn't have to change later. The guns were fairly loud and frequent to our right and left. It seemed quiet enough in front.

We went through a lot of wet woods full of leaflets in German asking: 'Where is the Luftwaffe?' and advising the Germans to surrender. Somewhere in front of us and below was the Trigno, and as the sun rose we saw the distant hills beyond. Those hills were held by the English. 'One more river, one more river to cross.'

Coming over the ridge, we saw a road twisting below us, and suddenly an air-raid started behind us. Two lorries halted till it was over. We walked on through the fields and met a boy, who told us that two bridges about half a mile on the road were guarded by Germans; presumably they were mined.

Going down a ditch to the road, we came across a horse tethered and with some straw bedding. It looked like a charger, but its saddle was covered with a rug. We left hurriedly. Then down another ditch, and as we went under the culvert beneath the road we heard a voice to our left cursing loudly in German. The ditch widened to a stream and we continued down it, leaving Belmonte on our right, quite close, and, farther off, Agnone. We stopped to eat some bread and cheese given us by the girls at lunch the day before, and discovered then that Peter had lost the knife. It didn't matter much—today must be decisive. I described army rations to Peter—porridge and bacon for breakfast, a meagre lunch, and the joys of bully stew in the evening.

Then we heard someone coming, and went on, leaving Peter's cheese behind.

We passed a dead mule, the whole of its backside blown out by a heavy-calibre revolver bullet. Two days ago someone had fired at us with one of those. We met a peasant family picking fruit, looking like apples and tasting like plums, from a tree resembling a rowan. Their advice agreed with what we had been told—if we kept in the stream bed we were safe. The stream widened almost to a river, and its villages were further from the banks as they grew steeper. In some places they were sheer cliffs of perhaps two hundred feet. Everywhere there were gardens, and we picked tomatoes and figs and apples for the first time for days. Summer seemed to linger on here. Everyone knew who we were and came to greet us. Piedmont seemed to them a long way off, down here in the foot of the Abruzzi.

Peter's boots were practically off, and he found walking on the steep slopes of the ploughed fields hard enough, but the river bed was of stones. At last he suggested we stop for lunch, but we were soon off again. It was the advantage of being two—one would always drive the other on. We kept to the stream bed; high above was the village Schiavi d'Abruzzi—there were Germans there; Germans in all the villages but none in this valley, so everyone said: 'Keep to the stream and you're safe.'

About twelve o'clock we met a man who told us that in half an hour we would be across the Trigno and that there were German posts on that side, too. In five hours he said we would be in the British lines.

While we walked, a dog came out barking and nipped Peter in the leg, ripping his new trousers. At last our stream joined the Trigno, a wide but shallow river. Beyond the hills which people said were held by the Germans was a wooded crest held by the English. We were both naturally in a great state of suspense, but I don't think we ever doubted that Providence would see us through. Everything had worked out so well all the way down. We now stopped and asked at each house. 'We could get a guide,' we were told, 'but he lived two miles off—he had taken seventeen people through the night before—there was no line.' Surely if he could go through with such a large party at night we two could do it by day. It was then about two o'clock.

We went on.

'It was possible to get through—there was a road the Germans used—that was the town of Trivento, the Germans were there and their next post was perhaps eight hundred yards up the hill in that wood.'

'One could get through dressed as we were—we looked like peasants—it would be better if we had hoes and looked as if we were going to work.'

One of the people to whom we spoke, a Roman evacuee, took us a little way and showed us where to cross the road running from Trivento along the ridge to the West; we decided to leave Trivento on our left.

We passed a cabin and went into the yard. There was no one there. I found a hoe and put a hundred-lire note in the keyhole.

We went across the road; in the next valley was a dry stream bed. 'Once across that, you're safe.' 'The Germans never go beyond it.' It was perhaps six hundred yards away. Oh, God! We had crossed the road almost on the edge of the town. Peter was perhaps two hundred yards ahead. He stopped to ask some peasants who were at work, and I, shouldering my hoe, walked past him for some way and stopped at another group. Peter was told: 'Oh, you'll easily cross now.' 'Just between that olive grove on the bend and that high cliff above the stream bed, that's where the posts are.' The two were perhaps five hundred yards apart.

I took my last piece of bread from my pocket and ate it as I walked across the stream. It wasn't very wide and it was bone dry. 'Once you're across, you're safe.' I didn't follow Peter's tracks; he turned into the nearest house and I walked on till I came to a field, where, fully conscious of the fact that I was still well within range of the German machine guns, I started to hoe.

When Peter caught me up, he handed me a piece of bread and cheese which the woman of the house had given him. She had offered to put us up for the night, and she lived only twenty-five yards from the German 'line'. It was getting dusk now; we had done the last two miles very slowly indeed.

It was a long way to the wood yet, and I felt our welcome at a section post would not be very friendly if they were suspicious of our coming at night; and, anyhow, they would have no blankets for us.

We were coming near some farms, and Peter said: 'How extraordinary that for the last sixty miles we haven't seen a single German!' Then, seeing the house, he suggested going into it to ask where the English were. I saw some men driving some goats towards us, perhaps thirty yards away, so I said: 'Let's ask them—it'll save time.' Peter said: 'I think they've got rifles'; and I: 'Yes, they're Germans.'

We turned off the track into the farm pretty smartly, nipped round the back and ran below the crest to the next one. It was a German foraging patrol. They never got rations and lived entirely off the country. At the next farm we were told that it was very rare for Germans to come on this side. The man, who had been to America, gave us some strong red wine, very good spongy white bread and a lot of hard cheese. We celebrated and had three glasses each. He offered to put us up, but we preferred to go further away. We gave him my hoe, and his wife our matches, needle and cotton and our piece of string, and set off very gaily.

By the time we reached the beginning of the wood we were tired; the idea of looking in dark woods for a post that had only consisted of two armoured cars seemed unattractive. Tonight we would have minestrone and wine and sleep in the hay, then porridge for breakfast, and an early start in the morning. We knocked on the door of the nearest house—it was dark by now—and went in. They were having minestrone. We couldn't eat our third helping, and drank lots of water out of the ladle from the bucket on the shelf. Our shoes were dried by the fire, and we talked; the son was an escaped soldier. They were a very dark family, and the father told me they were from Naples, so I asked him when they moved to the Abruzzi. He replied that his family had never moved, that this part of the Kingdom of Naples had been incorporated recently in the Abruzzi. We had come a long way from Piedmont to the Kingdom of Naples: Liguria—Aemilia—Tuscany—Umbria—Marche—Lazio—Abruzzi—and always the same kindness, the same welcome.

The barn was full of maize leaves, and we were lent blankets. A farm-boy came in and slept there with us.

### Forty-eighth Day
### 30th October, 1943

WE WERE, for once, astir before the household, but the old man wouldn't let us go without breakfast, and made his daughter fry us an egg each in green peppers. He insisted on coming with us, taking an axe with him, but took a long time saddling his mule and filling his bag with maize and potatoes. Oh, we were impatient! And he stopped and greeted everyone he met. A man said that the British had withdrawn from the wood, and it was some way to the nearest post. He would come with us.

We said goodbye to our Neapolitan host and followed the new man, who was an ex-Carabiniere from Trivento, well-dressed and a fast walker, through the wood. He told us not to talk, as German patrols were about. We didn't believe him, but we kept quiet. When we were clear of the wood, he started to tell us atrocity stories about the Germans, but we weren't listening much. We had about six miles to walk that morning; it was very muddy, and Peter, his wretched canvas boots discarded at last, was walking barefoot. There were a lot of people about, and at a small house the man left us. 'One kilometre down the track, and you will be there.' Peter and I, in spite of all the charity we had received, had each been of the opinion that both the Neapolitan and this man were coming with us, solely to get the reward for bringing us through. It was rather a shaming thought, after all the Italians had done for us, that we should still doubt their motives.

Then we were going downhill, and it was we and not the Italians who were saying: 'Where are the English?'

We came to a village, Lucita, spotlessly clean. We went down the steps of the village street; obviously the RAMC had been at work here. 'Where are the English headquarters?' we asked in the main street. 'In there.' We went in, and asked a man if he spoke English. No, he didn't. 'Are you two escaped prisoners?' said a voice from a chair. It was a barber's shop and there was a Canadian officer being shaved.

Later a sergeant took us down the road a bit—we still had some five miles to walk, and, after all, a river to cross. The bridge was blown, but the Delectable Mountains were in sight. Then we were walking down the road, high, wide and handsome—never seen the sun shine so bright—all this, and heaven, too. I knew what a million dollars felt like! We could look at the view now, at the mountains, the clouds and the sun—we could walk on roads in peace. I turned to Peter and said: 'We've done it!'

The holiday was over. That evening we were in battledress.

# AFTERWORD

THE STORY I NOW TELL is the fruit of three sons' researches into their fathers' wartime experiences – my own, Andrew Adams's and those of Ian Chard, whose father was captured with mine in the desert behind German lines in 1942.

I grew up on the story of my father's escape, of how Italian families had fed them and how they had to stay away from the larger villages where they were likely to be betrayed. For my father, the seven-hundred-mile journey through Italy was the adventure of his life.

Frank Simms's dream had always been to be a writer – he wrote two unpublished novels. His strong-minded mother thought otherwise. It was to be the familiar pattern: first son, navy – the senior service – second son, army and third, if there was one, the church.

My mother told me that after his return from Italy, he began to write down the story, detailing not only the long walk but his actual escape which took place a week before he teamed up with Peter Medd. Then, a letter arrived out of the blue from Peter Medd's family. Peter had been tragically killed just months after he escaped. My father was asked if he would complete Peter's escape diary, to be published as a memorial to him.

According to my mother, my father was deeply upset as this pre-empted his hopes of publishing his own account of his adventurous escape. But dutifully he completed Peter Medd's account and the story of their long walk together was published in February 1951 (with a second impression in April). Frank

Simms's name was not on the cover of the book, relegated to the title page.

*

My memories of my father are vivid but intermittent. He had been dispatched to Palestine weeks before I was born in September 1944 and had been in Ankara for just over a year as Senior Assistant Military Attaché when he was killed in a motor crash on September 3rd, 1952, when I was still just seven years old.

My cousin Blake Simms, son of my father's elder brother Hugh Crofton Simms, has some vivid memories of his uncle. The two brothers were apparently highly competitive. Hugh was a keen and successful sportsman, my father more the intellectual and the school chess champion at Malvern College. Yet my father was determined to keep up with his elder brother. Hugh joined the Navy aged fourteen, following in the footsteps of *his* father, and passed out of the Naval Training College, Dartmouth in 1924. My father took the entrance exam to Dartmouth and passed, says Blake. But he did not take the place up as he wanted to go to Oxford, though he was pressed instead by his family to join the Army.

My father had the reputation for being fearless. David Lloyd Owen, his comrade-in-arms in North Africa, described him as 'one of the few people I knew who really did not appear to know the meaning of fear.' Recalling his behaviour in action Blake recalls 'Uncle Frank would attack at every opportunity. He could think up incredible lines of attack and would never take no for an answer.'

Some months before she died in 1985, my mother started to write down her memories of my father so that I and my family should have a record of his life as far as she could recall.

The urge has come to set down what I can remember about Frank's part in the War as there is not much record of his gallantry.

His mother was Irish. Her name was Muriel
Crofton and Marcus and I called her Moonie. She was
a most amusing character and full of fascinating stories.

Of my grandfather Capt. Henry William Simms RN I heard
little. My cousins have copies of an award he was granted in
1911 by the King of Italy. In March that year he was created
a Commendatore (Commander) dell'Ordine della Corona
d'Italia, for services in the rescue of survivors of the devastating
1908 earthquake in Catania, Sicily. He died in 1951.

My mother continues:

Moonie loved the luxuries of life, good food and good
wine, but perhaps her greatest pleasure was reading after
breakfast… She had three children, Mary, Crofton and
Francis known as Frank. Money was short and she sent
Crofton into the Navy and Frank to Sandhurst. He
longed to go to Oxford, peacetime military life was not
his métier as we shall see. He made one effort to escape
that I remember him telling me about. He wrote home
and said he had a problem, he could not march in time
to music, no coordination. His elder brother Crofton
was sent down to see him by his Ma and told him that
he damned well had to solve the difficulty as there was
no alternative. Poor Frank, he got through it and joined
the Royal Warwickshire Regiment, and how he loathed
the boring routine. As soon as he saw a notice on the
board asking for volunteers to go to Spain and join
the Spanish Army on an exchange basis for a year he
rushed to the Adjutant to apply. Anything to get away
from this deathly routine on a 2nd Lieutenant's pay. He
set off for an adventure and greatly enjoyed the lack of
discipline, the weather and the wine. He learnt to speak
Spanish and the whole project was a success.

This was in 1933 – his service record gives brief details: 'Attached to the Spanish Army and served with 17 Regiment, Malaga.'

He returned invigorated but sadly there were the same old parades and dull mess dinners. Suddenly, Oh Joy, another notice went up on the board, this time asking for volunteers for the Sudan Defence Force. Again he succeeded and sailed away for the excitement of Suez and on down to Khartoum and the wilds of the desert in the Sudan.

The next part of the account was written by John Hood, a friend of my mother's who had served with Frank in the Sudan:

I have found a number of patrol reports and enclose one dated March 30th 1935 which is signed by Bimbashi (Officer) F. C. Simms Eastern Arab Corps. It would appear that Frank joined the Eastern Arab Corps in 1934.

After being selected for the Sudan Defence Force Frank would have reported to HQ Troops, Sudan, in Khartoum and from there Officers (Bimbashia) would have been posted to either Western Arab Corps in the far west of Sudan, Eastern Arab Corps on the Sudan/ Abyssinian frontier, Equatorial Corps down in the bogs of the Southern Sudan or Camel Corps in the Nuba Mountains. In addition we also had companies of artillery and engineers and signals etc.

I loved the Eastern Arab Corps very much. The work largely consisted of patrolling the Eastern Sudan frontier with Eritrea and Abyssinia. In peace time when Frank was there it was great fun, no real danger except the odd skirmish with ivory poachers and there were plenty of big game, including leopard, lion and the odd herd of elephant. Most of us liked being out on trek permanently, but every now and again one had to return to HQ which was a place called Gedaref, a dull dreary dusty little town with nothing much to commend it except polo and of course training the soldiery.

I had a batman called Musa from the Beni Amer Tribe in Eritrea who had served with Frank and knew him well. The officers all had their own small houses or their own rooms in the Battalion Mess buildings… As regards to the language, we all had to learn Arabic. We had to speak it pretty well. It took me about 6 months but it was not necessary to write it.

My mother took up the story:

I well remember that in peacetime Frank was awfully pleased to have his own house and servants. He loved the polo and he had a bookseller in Pall Mall to keep him supplied with books. He always spoke with much admiration of the Sudanese who served under him. The pay was much better than at home so he was able to save money to spend on leave.

His Regimental journal *The Antelope* adds an amusing note. 'Lt Col Simms in Khartoum with the 2nd Battalion in 1930 and afterwards with the SDF. His local knowledge has proved of great value, knowing as he does practically everyone in Khartoum from District Commissioners to the lowliest private in the SDF.'

Further vivid details of my father's service in the SDF are provided in John Orlebar's *The Story of the Sudan Defence Force*, an informal two-volume history. Orlebar served in the SDF and both were mentioned in despatches published in the London Gazette in April 1941.

My father, Orlebar wrote, was Officer-in-Command of No. 5 Motor Machine Gun [MMG] company, Eastern Arab Corps, SDF. His number two was Pat Cousens. The District Commissioner in Kassala, Andrew Blaikie, kept a diary which is cited in Orlebar's book. He wrote 'Frank was pale, fair haired and inclined to be cynical. A good brain and an excellent organiser. Very popular with his men. I liked him immensely and we fitted in well together. Pat was dark and handsome, a dashing subaltern 'a-raring to go'.'

Blaikie's entry for June 12th, 1940, runs:

5:35 a.m. Three Italian Caproni III's appeared from the East following the telegraph poles from Sabderat to Kassala. The company was heavily bombed, 58 bombs fell on the landing ground, five in Frank's house, 15 on the Fort and several on the Mirghani quarter. Planes were flying about 5000 feet in bad formation and turned back over Kassala and machine-gunned the town. No military casualties but about 10 persons wounded in the Mirghani quarter – three seriously.

On June 14 he continued:

The Sudan is now officially at war with Italy!! Army off at 4:30a.m. Up at 5.30, had tea and worked in the garden. Two Italian planes passed over at 7a.m. but dropped no bombs – they were looking for the army.

Frank to breakfast, then across to Kassala about 9 a.m. there are many things to be done – reopening of souk, control of prices, punishment of profiteers, digging an adequate amount of air raid trenches, organisation of supplies, personal worries, wages, police patrols and army liaison, cyphers, grain distribution, the packing and dispatch of the household goods of the Province

Headquarters staff ... the interrogation of agents, deserters of Eritrea, refugees and suspects, control of petrol and transport and finally the continual interviewing of notables, officials and ordinary people and the calming of the troubled hearts of all. And the news is just bloody...

June 18:

Seems odd to be carrying on war and yet all the time enjoying all the pleasures of this station – like fighting the enemy in the morning outside one's own castle, and then retiring in the afternoon to sleep and enjoy oneself.

Further diary entries record frequent skirmishes – June 24th 'Frank did a useful patrol to Ali Ghidder killing about 15 of the enemy.'

Blaikie recalls that on June 27th he was in the lavatory, meditating before breakfast, when the telephone rang. Frank's voice said 'the Campbells are coming' and rang off. This evidently meant the enemy was upon them. Blaikie hurriedly changed from pyjamas into his uniform, buckled on his revolver and rushed in the car across the River Gash into Kassala. In town there was chaos. Army cars were rushing about and everybody was standing out in the streets. Reaching the office he learnt from my father that an attack was imminent. Joining my father's field HQ he heard the news that two of his Motor Machine Gun cars had met about 150 enemy cavalry advancing down the Saberat-Kassala road. These were a screen for a much larger force behind. Blaikie wrote:

The leading cavalry were routed with considerable loss. Our cars chased them back onto the main body and killed 14 with revolvers at close range, besides mowing down a great many more with machine gun fire. The main body evidently retreated as soon as our reinforcements arrived on the scene. A great victory and we all had a terrific reception as we returned with captured equipment to the souk.

Later it emerged from records captured at Addis Ababa that nearly two thousand Italians were killed, while British losses amounted to three. The greater part of the Italian casualties were inflicted by the armoured cars of the Engineer Troops who caught motorised infantry advancing along the west bank of the river. They set alight and destroyed twenty-three heavy lorries and all the passengers.

After an initial defeat resulting in a withdrawal from Kassala, Imperial and French forces pushed back and into Eritrea, Italian Somaliland and Ethiopia, forcing the Italians to surrender in November 1941.

*

My father was posted to the Long Range Desert Group on September 1st, 1941. The background to the formation of the LRDG is sketched by General Sir John Hackett in his foreword to *Providence Their Guide* (1980) by Major General David Lloyd Owen.

In World War II the Mediterranean Theatre offered an almost embarrassing choice of open flanks. There was not only the sea with enormous stretches of coastline, often backed by useful mountains, there was also the desert. The land battle for Africa, and for control of the Southern shore of the Mediterranean, was essentially fought along a narrow coastal strip, a couple of thousand miles long but rarely more than fifty deep. To the south lay vast stretches of desert wasteland, little visited and largely unexplored. In these deserts there came into being one of the most remarkable of the small specialist forces spawned in such numbers and variety by the British in the Mediterranean theatre of war. This was the Long Range Desert Group.

It was in deep reconnaissance, among many other distinguished activities, that the LRDG shone with truly unrivalled brilliance. A circuitous journey, often over a thousand miles long, would bring a patrol well inside hostile territory to a point where a couple of men with binoculars would be hidden a few hundred yards away from the main Axis supply road. There they would stay, counting every vehicle, in any category, which went up or down and reporting the tally back to GHQ. The value of this information in the attempt to divine the enemy's intentions was quite incalculable. The skill and boldness with which it was obtained take the breath away.

The founder and first commander of the LRDG was Brigadier Ralph Alger Bagnold FRS OBE (1896-1990). The unit was formed in Egypt in June 1940 under Field Marshal Wavell. The majority of the men were initially from New Zealand, soon joined by Southern Rhodesian and British volunteers. David Lloyd Owen explains:

After France had collapsed Italy declared war on us on June 10th, 1940. Overnight the whole strategic picture altered and the dangers which Bagnold had seen so clearly were now something that they had to face, for if Marshal Graziani decided to march into Egypt with his quarter of a million men he would have only taken three days to reach the Nile. Bagnold presented his report again and on June 23rd he was summoned to see General Wavell. He writes that the C-in-C grinned at the scheme. Then he suddenly asked him if he could be ready in 6 weeks! He signed what amounted to a blank cheque empowering Bagnold to order anything he wanted as an absolute priority from any department in Egypt, with no questions to be asked.

At the end of August, seen off by Wavell himself, the LRDG with three patrols, each of two officers and 28 men, moved off in secrecy from Cairo. Their task was to harass the Italians in any part of Libya they chose and to draw their troops and transport (of which they were short) away from the coastal region to the defence of scattered garrisons in the deep interior...

Graphic detail of my father's service with the LRDG is provided in two letters to my mother from my father's navigator Mike 'Lofty' Carr:

I was not of course allowed to keep a full account of our doings, my jottings being surviving scraps of notes made mainly in my capacity as your late husband's navigator and because I am a competitive note-taker... The anecdotes will tend to have a light touch. He had an impish sense of humour, behind his somewhat formal front. You must bear with me if I refer to him as Captain Simms. That is how we all addressed him and how I think of him.

There is little mention of actual offensive action against the enemy but many insights into how the LRDG operated. The terrain was very difficult to traverse, but they became adept at it, so even when the Germans were close and had them in view the enemy could not easily pursue them. Ravines and scrub provided many good hiding places, especially when camouflage nets were in place. By contrast when moving, whether singly or in convoy, they were very easily spotted from the air by both Luftwaffe and RAF aircraft. And though they had some impressive success in persuading German planes they were Axis vehicles, the response of the RAF proved terrifyingly different on at least one occasion.

In the second letter to my mother, Lofty took up the story:

We called him 'carry-on-Simms' because whenever confronted by some obstacle which would have caused other men to deviate or postpone or even abandon a project he always said the same thing, viz: 'Burgess – is the Vickers loaded?' (Corporal Burgess, ex Middle-East Commando, his gunner)... 'Carr - where are we?' ... 'It's alright: they've not seen us.' ... (They often had): 'We'll carry on.'

For example the Germans had an airfield 13 miles long called Martuba. It lay in our path and I suggested a detour to get round it. He said his classic 'They won't see us.' He set off across it right in its middle. I think that this was when an anti-tank gun put a solid shell through his truck, which we were towing with mine. The shell took the bottom out of Captain Simms enamel mug which was hanging by his left shoulder. He was very amused and liked showing people his mug.

Lofty continued:

That night we were creeping our trucks slowly away in steep hill country when an enemy patrol found us in their searchlight beam. We stopped and at this point Captain Simms started complaining that he had lost his old greatcoat, to which he was most attached. 'Had it since I joined the Army,' he went on, the searchlight still on us. 'It was on my truck a moment ago.' He hopped off his truck and walked back the way we had come using the light from the enemy to help him search. He found it, walked back to his truck and we got away. I think that his calm reaction made the enemy hold their fire, thinking that we were 'some of them' (this happened on a number of occasions).

My father and Lofty shared a keen interest in nature. Lofty recalled:

He was as you know a fierce and determined soldier but very soft hearted about birds etc. There were a lot migrating across the desert. He found one dead by an empty petrol tin and was almost reduced to tears. 'That poor little bird' he said, 'it has been walking up and down by this tin 'waiting for death'.'

He beckoned me on one occasion, well behind the enemy lines; he seemed excited. Quickly I followed him wondering what he had discovered. It turned out to be a load of desert flowers, rather like Livingstone daisies. These had sprung up as happens in deserts overnight following a rainstorm. We spent some time enjoying the sight.

My father's arrival as commander of Y Patrol brought a rapid change to daily routine.

The first morning he took over Y he had us all out of bed at dawn to play netball. We couldn't believe our ears. I suppose like all young soldiers, we thought we were pretty tough. His version of the game was different. If one grabbed the ball Captain Simms usually knocked you flying. We soon learned and a cross between rugby and unarmed combat evolved. We were surprised at his agility because he seemed to us to be a great deal older than we were.

My father, says Lofty, spoke Italian as well as Arabic.

On one occasion we captured an enemy post office. Captain Simms put on a very comic act, much to our surprise as he read the mail aloud to us. He was always joking that we should try and capture an Italian paymaster next time so as to get all the cash.

His own personal favourite weapon was an Italian tommy gun which he had acquired [The one that let him down when he was captured]. It had a short bayonet on it.

My father was conscientious and trained his men at every opportunity. Lofty gives an example from their November '41 patrol:

He never wasted an opportunity to train me on our patrols on foot. E.g.: he and I had left the trucks hidden in high ground and were walking down a valley leading to the plain where a large number of enemy could be seen. We wanted a close look at what they were up to. On the way down the valley he gave me a detailed lecture on the techniques and theories of creeping down valleys in enemy country. He made it sound like a practice. I think it was his way of reassuring me. In the event when we reached the enemy we watched them playing football for a while (I've not been to a football match since!) had a look at some marquees they were using and planned to attack them that night. When we got back to the trucks there was a signal telling us to go somewhere else immediately.

My father's manner of leadership was firm but quiet-spoken. Lofty notes 'I did not hear him swear on any occasion. I did not hear him reprimand anyone nor raise his voice. He did however demand and get absolute obedience.'

Having lived for nearly ten years in northern Africa my father was keen to point out local customs and manners. In a brief chronology Lofty sent to my mother he notes the following incidents:

22.10.41
Y patrol is to be divided, myself to be with Captain Simms, went with him to HQ re navigation methods. On way back Captain Simms drew our attention to a gathering of natives in the middle of the village. We stopped and he explained that it was a dance (stick dance) celebrating release from slavery...
25.10.41
PT and ' netball' early morning! Took Captain Simms on theodolite in morning and was told interesting tales by him of his time in Spain, Sudan, Italy, Abyssinia and France. I am finding Oasis life more interesting as run by Captain Simms on organised lines, than previously.
8.11.41
Reached Siwa. (Captain Simms training us on mortars etc)
14.11.41
Left Siwa (To play our part behind enemy lines in the November push (Operation Crusader, intended to push the Axis out of Libya))

On November 16th came a terrifying incident as RAF planes spotted them in open desert. Lofty gives brief details: 'Five miles from our objective we were attacked by three Beaufort fighters (RAF). Recognition signals failed; they hit every truck. Mine, the radio truck, went up in smoke (with Captain

Simms and myself beneath it trying to light a recognition flyer unsuccessfully). Managed to save papers (by sneaking back up in the dark, despite heavy rain).'

On November 23rd came new orders – the patrol was to take on a role akin to that of the nascent SAS under David Stirling. 'Radio message changed our role from recce to 'violent offensive action' (which was what Captain Simms had been pressing for).'

Enemy aircraft continued to be a problem. On November 25th Lofty noted, 'Machine gunned half-heartedly by a Heinkel. Back (early) evening and I found a good funk hole for a read.'

The next day Lofty was on a ten-mile foot-recce with my father. 'We were crossing a temporary lake eighteen inches deep pestered by aircraft, to our embarrassment as we could not, of course, lie down.'

Two days later they were preparing to launch an attack on Luftwaffe planes at Martuba airport. 'Captain Simms and I went on five-mile foot-recce to a valley full of enemy engaged in PT and football.' They noted a range of vehicles and what appeared to be well-dug-in marquees. 'Captain Simms intends attacking them tomorrow night. Reached our trucks in darkness.'

The next day, November 29th, they moved their vehicles up to the head of the valley, but just as they moved into place for the assault they received an order on the radio to attack the main (coast) road.

> Moved at midday and crawled the trucks to South edge of Martuba Airdrome. Were crossing it when Captain Simms's truck stalled and would not restart. At this moment an enemy ground patrol spotted him. I took him in tow with my truck and we headed south like the clappers as fighter planes began taking off like bees. We dived the trucks into shallow wadis in a great dust cloud

which concealed us from diving 109s as the setting sun threw long shadows. In darkness we drove slowly south being intercepted by enemy ground patrols with searchlights. Stopped 2030 hours.

The military actions which Lofty had only alluded to are described in more detail in *Special Forces in the Desert War: 1940–1943*, published by the National Archives in 2001. The new orders, mentioned by Lofty and dated November 24th 1941, ordered the group 'to act with the utmost vigour offensively against any enemy targets or communications within reach.'

On December 2nd at about 7pm, in the neighbourhood of Abier-el-Aleima, my father's patrol, Y1, found itself in the middle of an enemy MT (Mechanical Transport) park of about thirty vehicles. They were able to damage fifteen of them before withdrawing; but it was found that navigator Lance Corporal Carr was missing and though the patrol waited at the first rendezvous he did not reappear.

This was the week when the LRDG drove David Stirling across the desert to his now legendary attack on an enemy airfield at Tamet, where Paddy Mayne destroyed twenty-four aircraft, a petrol dump and a bomb, and a house containing about forty of the enemy was 'soundly shot up'.

According to his war diary, Lofty found a camp of the Senussi Bedouin clan where he was sheltered and fed for a fortnight, while the battle went on all around him. By December 17th, British troops were advancing and he and a wounded RAF officer to whom the Senussi had also given shelter were picked up by the 31st Field Regiment RA, and taken to the HQ of the 4th Indian Division. Lofty reached Siwa on December 23rd. In his memoirs written for my mother he wrote 'Re-united with Y and Captain Simms. He told me to write home.'

Three days later he noted: 'Arabs all very excited all night. Captain Simms told me each family kills a sheep and the village as a whole slaughter a camel for this feast.' The following three days he adds: 'Experimenting with new mortar tactics on sand with Colonel Prendergast and Captain Simms also extra revolver practice with Titch Cave prior to move in with Captain Simms to Gialo.' Gialo was an oasis and another of their advance bases.

On January 2nd Lofty evokes the perennial dream of those in the desert for a cold beer, which is a theme of the famous 1958 film *Ice Cold in Alex* about an escape through classic LRDG desert terrain. Lofty recalls: 'Had a can of ale from Captain Simms for my lunch! In the desert en route from Siwa to Gialo.'

My father was captured in Libya on January 13th, 1942. 'The Germans could never understand how the British ventured so far into enemy territory,' my mother told me.

*

When a soldier goes missing his family is faced with an agonising wait for news – is he alive, wounded or captured? My mother received the news in a postcard from Frank's mother dated March 7th, 1942. Moonie wrote: 'I now know Frank is alive. Wounded and a prisoner of war.'

A second postcard from Moonie followed on March 20th:

> Frank was shot through the thigh and in the left hand. He was taken prisoner when he and one man, a sergeant, were on a reconnaissance… They climbed a cliff nearly 300ft as soon as dawn broke and once up were doing their work (only the two of them) when three lorries with sixty-six men raced at them through a gap in the hills. They were too far on the plateau to get back and down the escarpment so they stood and fired their tommy guns… Frank's gun jammed and not one shot could it fire.

My father had written from a German hospital in Libya and said he was 'quite comfy and nothing permanent and no pain [and] was well looked after,' adding that he 'has suffered no permanent injury at all.'

My mother's recollections in 1985 were similar but slightly different:

> Frank told me all about his capture. He and his sergeant set off to watch this village above which were many salt pillars [These were distinctive steep flat topped hills rising sheer from the desert floor]. They climbed up one of these to lie and watch all the movements in the village to try to gauge the numbers of troops, war vehicles and artillery. Through his field glasses he saw a large staff car drive up towards them, it stopped nearby and a chap got out... He looked around for a salt pillar to climb, choosing the very one that Frank was occupying. As his head drew level with the top he saw the muzzle of Frank's rifle pointing at him. Frank fired but the breech was full of sand and it failed to go off. The astonished German slid down and Frank and his sergeant dropped down the other side and ran for it. They were both shot in the leg, captured and taken to a German hospital. There they were treated very well indeed. Frank said that to his surprise they were even given sweets like the German patients. He also said the Germans seemed frightfully impressed with the LRDG as they themselves never worked behind our lines and never in small patrols...

Further enthralling detail comes from my father's companion on the recce, Trooper Harry Chard – via his son Ian who has diligently pursued his own researches of his father's wartime service and capture. Though my father and Harry Chard were captured at the same time, they were separated soon after and neither knew what had happened to the other till after the war.

Chard had rejoined my father's Y1 Patrol early in the New Year of 1942, when he was still not fully recovered from dysentery. Hearing the patrol was short of a machine gunner he had volunteered.

Our instructions were to go to Fort Marada (about sixty miles inland from El Agheila) and find out if it was still occupied by the enemy, as the RAF had reported that it was unoccupied. When about ten miles from Marada, we found that we could not advance any nearer with the trucks because of a steep escarpment down to the floor of the wadi. Captain Simms decided to leave the patrol here while he went on to the fort on foot, taking me with him as an escort. I left all of my personal kit with my driver, Bill Bullock, and we set off down the escarpment. We had our water bottles and only a small pack of hard biscuits, as we did not expect to be away for very long. However, the country was far rougher than we had anticipated. Presently night overtook us and we had to sleep in the sand dunes without blankets or overcoats as we had to travel light. It was very cold and we had to huddle together to keep warm.

At sunrise on January 13th we had our breakfast of water and biscuits and set off towards the fort. The sand dunes finished about one hundred yards before the fort, so we were able to get quite close. We could not see any movement for a while, but then a couple of army trucks came out and drove up and down the track. We discovered later that they were learning to drive, which was bad luck for us. One truck stopped at the base of our dune and the driver got out and climbed up the dune. He obviously spotted our footprints and wondered whose they were. When his head appeared over the top and he saw us, Captain Simms shouted at him in Italian, but unfortunately this did not work and he shot at us but missed.

Captain Simms then lunged at him with his bayonet, shouting to me to shoot the Jerry with my revolver, but it wouldn't fire because of the sand in it. The Jerry ran away and now that we were discovered we tried to escape. Because of all the shooting more soldiers came out of the fort, and when they saw us running away opened fire on us, wounding Captain Simms in the thigh. He went down, shouting that he was shot. I ran back to help him, but he gasped to me to try to get back to our patrol. I jumped up and ran zigzagging but the bullets were flying thick and fast, so I dived to the ground and Jerry just surrounded us and took us prisoners.

The Germans treated us surprisingly well, gave us coffee and spoke to us in English. Captain Simms's wound was treated, and then we were put in a car to be taken to Rommel's headquarters to be interrogated. They must have known we were LRDG and kept on asking us questions, to which we only replied with our names, ranks and numbers. Field Marshal Rommel was not there, so we saw his second-in-command. From there we were taken to a fighter aerodrome, but on the way, we were attacked by British fighter planes. The Jerries dived out of the car for shelter and so did we! It was ironic but we all had a good laugh.

When we arrived at the aerodrome we were both taken to the officers' mess and given a meal, then Captain Simms was taken to hospital and I did not see him again during the war.

Harry Chard was handed over to a convoy, and later on to an Italian convoy which was on its way to Tripoli. On arrival at Miserata, he was taken to a field hospital because 'on our long walk I had worn boots instead of chapplis, or sandals, which they usually wore in the desert, causing my feet to become badly blistered ... From there I was taken to the POW holding camp at Fort Tarhuna. I was able to send a letter home from here via the Red Cross, just telling them that I was safe and being treated well by the Ities and Jerries.'

In 2007 Ian Chard embarked on a remarkable journey in search of the point of capture near Marada Oasis. Here he found a form of table mountain, flat-topped and rising sheer from the desert below. He identified the likely route up for both our fathers and their captor. This was a steep path rising diagonally through the near vertical upper face of the rock.

During his research about his father, Ian Chard also made contact with the widow of Werner Kost, the German soldier who captured our fathers. Werner Kost wrote a book, *Gebirgsjäger in Libyens Wüste*, on his experiences in the North Africa campaign with Rommel's Afrika Corps. His description of the capture translates as follows:

> Aerial Reconnaissance had announced the 'LRDG' coming from the south. Mountain Troops (Gebirgsjäger) were ordered to occupy forward positions at the edge of the salt-lakes. The table mountains allowed a very good view which allowed us to await the LRDG calmly. Lt. Kost was driving to one of the table mountains whilst the 1st Platoon of his troops occupied positions at the edge of the oasis. Lt. Kost wanted to climb the hill to have a look down towards his troops' positions. Climbing up a gully, he glanced up and was suddenly looking into the barrel of the submachine gun of a British soldier kneeling in front of him. Klick – the

gun had jammed – his luck held. [It was Friday 13 January, 1942] Two British soldiers bolted up out of cover and leapt down in a great leap from the other side of the plateau into a sand hollow. Quick as lightning and as if well practised one of his men passed Kost a rifle. The British soldiers were running zigzag through the salt marshes. Kost took aim and hit one of them in the leg. As the two Germans came down to the wounded man cautiously and covering themselves the other British soldier came out of his hiding place with his hands up. The one hit by the rifle was Captain Simms. His companion was a sergeant-major. The Germans bandaged up the wounded British Captain and together they smoked a 'peace cigarette'. Captain Simms remained for a few days with the Germans and gave them his compass as a present…

Following the death of Kost's widow, Ian Chard received a copy of Kost's book. All this raises intriguing questions. Were the Germans as fully alerted to the LRDG's presence as claimed? Clearly they would have realised that Captain Simms and Sergeant-Major Chard (actually Trooper but Sergeant-Major would be a greater prize) had motor transport not far away from their observation post on the salt pillar – which might still be nearby awaiting their return from a recce.

Lofty Carr provides a further twist to the story in a letter to General Lloyd-Owen in June 1985. On January 12th, the day before the capture, he had carried out a first recce with my father:

Captain Simms and I carried out four (foot) recces in the afternoon, seeing a coral reef many interesting shell and fossils also, of course collecting military information. Later in the day moved trucks close (5 miles) to Marada. Captain Simms and Chard went (on foot in the dark) to recce (closer). I was left behind as Captain Simms wanted me to take some star shots.

The next day – the day of the capture – he waited all day having 'heard trucks and aircraft and one burst of firing.'

The next day they again waited all day for Simms and Chard at a second rendezvous. 'No Luck. Recce planes all day.' The day after, January 15th, while they 'remained (hidden) in position all day, the food and water situation compelled us to go.' The Germans, it seems, were mounting an aerial search and found nothing. Ian Chard's photographs show the rocky terrain, with crevasses and scrub in which the LRDG could concealed trucks as well as a stingray can hide itself in the sand on the seabed.

My father was transferred to Italy after his capture. On his arrival he was taken to the POW camp at Padula (PG35 on the Red Cross map of British prisoner of war camps), a large Carthusian monastery in Southern Italy superbly evoked by George Millar in his escape story *Horned Pigeon*.

Here my father met another LRDG comrade, Captain Richard Carr (no relation of Lofty), who was adjutant of the LRDG with fourteen men and seven vehicles. He was an unfortunate victim of Rommel's rapid counter attack which had begun on January 21th.

He and his men had left Gialo on January 24th to bring a load of petrol from Msus. As he had no wireless truck it was impossible to warn him of the enemy's rapid advance. When he arrived at Msus he found it in enemy hands and the whole party was taken prisoner. Later in the day, while they were being removed, the German convoy was attacked by two British armoured cars and seven men contrived to escape but Captain Carr and the other seven remained prisoners.

\*

Before he was killed in 1952, my father was able to tell one part of his adventures in his own words. This was a detailed description of his escape with twelve others from Padula, which was published in three parts in his Regimental Magazine *The Antelope*, the third being published shortly after his death in Turkey. The text of these articles can be found on page 221.

My father described Padula as 'probably the most beautiful prisoner of war camp in Europe… It was set in a fruitful and shining valley surrounded by mountains some 80 miles south-east of Salerno. It was a large building with honey-coloured walls and roofs of old and lichened tiles; in honour of its Patron Saint [St Lawrence] the building was shaped like a grid iron.'

He provides an enthralling description of digging the tunnel, on a par with the famous book and film *The Wooden Horse*. Here are all the fascinating details of how they hid the soil, how rotas were arranged for them to surface and clean up in time for roll calls, how they concealed the tunnel entrance from the ever-more-suspicious Italians and how, even after they escaped, their captors never discovered either the tunnel entrance or the exit.

The furore caused by the thirteen-man escape in a populous area inevitably meant they were recaptured, though three made it to the coast. Recapture meant they were transferred to the Colditz of North Italy, the Castello di Gavi south of Turin, known colloquially as 'the naughty boys' camp', from which none escaped until the Italians capitulated in 1943. It was here, of course, that Simms met Peter Medd.

\*

When Italy dramatically signed an armistice on September 3rd 1943 (promulgated on September 8th), the Italians opened the gates of the prison. According to my father there were three options… to walk out of the castle gates and make an immediate bid for freedom, though without papers or disguise this was risky. To hide in the castle and hope that German searches would not be too thorough. Both my father and Peter Medd chose the third option of attempting the escape as the Germans transferred them on to trains for Germany. (Interestingly I never heard mention of the 'Stay Put' order issued by MI9, instructing POWs to await the arrival of Allied forces. If such an order reached Gavi, it was evidently completely disregarded).

Peter Medd describes how he jumped from the train taking prisoners from Acqui to Alessandria where they were to be transferred to Turin and a secure train to Germany. My father escaped earlier, jumping from the convoy of open-top cattle trucks taking them to Acqui Terme. Each lorry had a machine gun nest on the top of the cab trained on the lorry in front and ready to gun down any one who tried to jump over the high sidings of the truck. I loved to hear the story.

In her memoir, my mother provides vivid details:

Frank took a quick decision not to hide in the cellars although he had made a cache of food just in case. He rushed to pack his kit bag and get down to the trucks early enough to pick one that would suit his purpose. His purpose being to escape on the journey. He found that each truck had high sides like hay carts and being early he managed to load his kit bag in a truck unseen with the idea that he could use it as a foothold should he be able to jump out. The orders were to load all personal belongings in one lorry but he got away with it.

Just as they were all ready to start, the Germans started running and shouting. The special seat reserved for the Brigadier who was c-in-c of the prisoners was empty. There was no sign of him. After more waiting, more consternation and more yelling, the whole convoy moved off. You can imagine how desperate they all felt, having been so near to escape and freedom. A deep depression showed on every face at the grim thought of a German prison awaiting them.

Frank was seething with thoughts and wild ideas as to the possibilities of escape. As each truck had a driver and a co-driver and another soldier on the roof with a machine gun pointed at the vehicle ahead, he quickly realised that the road must be going uphill so that they were driving more slowly. It would have to take place on a bend so that the gun behind would be out of firing range and there would have to be cover on his side of the road. It was September and the road was dry and very dusty, swirls of dust covered them all. On they went for miles, interminable miles. Just as he was beginning to dread failure they started to go uphill and 'my God' everything was there that he longed for. Using his kit bag as a mount he was up and over and running into the woods. He heard the screeching of brakes but for a few minutes there were no shots as the dust had filled the breech of the gun on the roof. As he ran he heard turmoil and shots being fired as the convoy came to a halt (This he heard later from friends).

My mother was writing from memory of what my father had told her many times. Long after her death I came across my father's own account in the National Archives, given in a debriefing session to army officers on his return. It is cryptic and brief, almost as if he was keeping the juicier details for a future occasion, but it confirms my mother's story. The report runs:

On 9 September the Germans took over the camp. On 13 September all of us were taken to Acqui station, except about fifty, including the Senior British Officer, who were hiding in various cellars (the camp was in an old castle). On the way to the station (we were travelling in MT) I managed to jump off my lorry.

There were 12 of us in it, and also, sitting on the roof of the driver's cab, were three Germans one had a TSMG and the other two rifles. The lorry was going at not more than 15 mph but his gun jammed. The lorry stopped and the tommy-gunner ran after me but I outstepped him. This was in daylight. I made my way towards River Pescara.

It sounds almost like the hand of providence. My father had been captured when his own gun had jammed in the desert, now he escaped thanks to his guard's gun also jamming.

My mother's narrative continues:

He went on running crashing through undergrowth and heard the distant noise of the convoy restarting. But he ran until his lungs gave out for he was not very fit after all these months in prison on poor food. He came to a little stream where he drank and then lay exhausted in some bracken. His mind half-crazed with the joy of freedom mixed with the worries as to what was happening to his friends together with the fear of being followed.

Suddenly he heard the noise of someone coming towards him, he lay absolutely still, almost paralysed with dread. Fortunately there was no need to panic for along the path sauntered a small boy.

Both were equally surprised, the boy, about eight years old, sat down beside him. He was thrilled to hear that he was an escaped English prisoner of war and even more excited about his method of escape. Frank told him that he intended to walk south along the Apennines to try and reach the British Army and that he was badly in need of a map and clothes. Above all he needed food for he was feeling very hungry. Antonio was his name and he entered into the conspiracy with tremendous enthusiasm. Telling Frank to stay exactly where he was he disappeared into the woods.

Frank fell asleep, exhausted by such an emotional day. He awoke to find a triumphant Antonio, who was carrying an old basket from which came an ancient cap to cover Frank's very fair hair, some dirty old trousers and a crumpled map.

Underneath these disguises nestled thirty raw eggs. Frank had never cooked anything in his life. He had no idea how to break an egg but he was so starving he squashed them in his hands and swallowed them as best he could with upmost nausea! Antonio was hysterical. He thought it the funniest thing he had ever seen. He put on the trousers, which fitted reasonably well, and gave his good warm khaki trousers in exchange and some lira. After a fond farewell he started walking in a southerly direction, little realising he would have to slog it for some seven hundred miles.

My mother continued:

I don't remember much about the next seven days but I will quote excerpts from Peter Medd's book as he was in the same prison and escaped from the train on the way to Germany. Peter told me that he chased after Frank wanting to catch up with him. He took the route that he knew Frank would take and asked along the way for a fair Englishman. He was walking with an Italian called Guiliano and I quote from the seventh day of his diary. 'Down the road from the muddy village of Baragelata (frozen beard) we passed a sailor carrying a kit bag on his shoulder, he, too, was walking home. He told us there was an Englishman staying at the Osteria, so we decided to investigate. Our enquiry was received with suspicion by the landlady but she went upstairs to report. Next a rather anxious face appeared at an upper window, to be transformed suddenly into a broad smile of recognition. It was Frank, who had escaped six hours before me from the lorry.'

Peter Medd met up with my father on their seventh day of freedom. His narrative continues till the twenty-eighth day (October 10th) when it is taken over by my father. Their route is broadly traceable from the names of villages towns and mountains they passed. Some, inevitably, are misspelt in the diary making them difficult to identify, but they marry up with places with similar names broadly on the west–east route they followed as they walked down the Apennines.

*

By chance, an extraordinary new window on to this journey has been opened by Andrew Adams, who is the initiator of this reprint of *The Long Walk Home*. He was prompted by his own father's escape from an Italian POW Camp. Through his interest in the Italian families who helped escaping Allied POWs, he made contact with the Abrami family who hold such a place of honour in the long list of Italians, who at huge risk to themselves, fed and hid Allied POWs. The Abramis, as Medd vividly describes, had lived in London for a decade before the war, bringing up their three daughters and son Frank in north London while running a flourishing café. With Mussolini bent on declaring war, they had returned to Italy rather than risk internment. Their heroic story is told in Frank Abrami's book *In the Shadow of the Gothic Line* (privately printed in 2014). As an eleven-year-old boy, Frank Abrami had risked his life bringing food to my father and Peter Medd for nearly a week while Peter recovered from illness.

He describes how my father and Peter, after twelve days of trekking along the Apennines, keeping clear of large towns and German patrols, were approaching the beautiful province of Garfagnana:

> Walking down the main road to Castelnuovo they ran into our very own Mr Webb, who called out from behind them 'Hello! You're Englishmen aren't you?'
>
> They both turned around and, to their amazement, saw a short bald-headed middle-aged man wearing plus fours and carrying a rucksack. He was accompanied by a very pretty young woman who turned out to be his wife and he introduced himself as Mr Webb, who had worked for the Shell company before the war. He went on to explain that at the outbreak of the war he had been interned, then released at the armistice and finally found himself living in Garfagnana. He had just moved into a small house with his Italian wife and child in a mountain village called Roggio further up from Castelnuovo.
>
> Mr Webb then invited them to accompany him to his home. They did not want to take the risk of walking into town and, hoping not to appear rude, wished him goodbye for now with a promise to meet up with him the following day. They had met a Mr Biagion (who had been an ice-cream seller in Glasgow before the war) earlier in the day and he had invited them to spend the night at his house on the outskirts of town where it would be safer. They managed to flag down a passing lorry which was full of children. The driver agreed to give them a lift and as the lorry trundled down the hill they took their leave of Mr Webb. They did not entirely trust him at this time, thinking it was more likely that he was a German agent; probably on a mission to befriend and facilitate the recapture of escaped prisoners of war travelling in

the hills of which there were many hundred all over Italy at this time.

As they sheltered out with Mr Biagion that night, the two escapees discussed their options. They had been so taken aback by meeting such an obvious Englishman in this part of Italy that they thought he must be an agent of the German Gestapo, placed there to ensnare any POWs like themselves. They were also suspicious as he had tried to dissuade them from immediately continuing their journey towards Allied lines and take the more passive approach of hiding in Roggio and awaiting the eventual arrival of friendly forces.

Peter Medd had been carrying an injury to his hip and was very aware he badly needed some rest before resuming the journey, so they finally decided to trust Webb and to rest in Roggio for a week or so. They met Mr Webb at 6.30 the next morning, half expecting him to be dressed in a Gestapo uniform and accompanied by armed guards that would take them back to prison. But their fears were calmed when they saw him waiting for them in his English tweeds, wearing a large rucksack in which he had packed food and other supplies that they would need during their stay. They were thankful that they had decided to trust him.

Together they walked up the main road to Roggio, then turned up a track which followed a valley into the heart of the hills. As they advanced into the deeper forest, they had time to observe and appreciate the landscape of cascading streams, ancient mills and vine-covered farmhouses. They asked Mr Webb whether there were people living in the small huts dotted throughout the forest with smoke rising out of them. He explained that they were called a Metato, and were for drying chestnuts. He told them that my father would probably hide them in one of the structures during their stay – there were so many of them that the Germans could not hope to search them all.

Frank Abrami continues:

While Medd and Simms spent the first night in Roggio, there was a meeting in our house involving my parents and several concerned villagers. The two Englishmen were not the first escaping POWs to be given assistance, but these two being officers some worried that they might be more actively pursued by the Germans. For the safety of Roggio's inhabitants, it was decided they should be moved to a hut that was more remote from the village, so that if the worst should happen and the men were captured, the villagers could deny any knowledge of them.

So early the next morning, Dad and Bruno guided them up to another shepherd's hut, right on the crest of the hills overlooking Roggio. Although it was higher up, at almost 3000 feet, this meant that it afforded a clear view down the steep slope of scree dotted with beech trees, which fell away on the far side of the ridge. Some 2000 feet below them, at the bottom of the slope, was the picturesque village of Vagli Sopra. Medd commented that it looked a charming spot, but Bruno warned him that there were German troops stationed in the village, so they must avoid going anywhere near it.

Behind Vagli Sopra reared a spectacular mountain mass, so sheer that it almost looked artificial. Dad told them that these were the Carrara Mountains, proudly adding that they were the source of the finest marble in the world.

Operations at the marble quarries had steadily wound down as the war advanced.

The group of men turned from admiring the mountains and inspected the new hut. It was only eight feet by eight and in a fairly poor state of repair, with many gaps in the walls. There were also two small outbuildings, or 'Capannas', mainly constructed of straw thatch. One was a sheep pen and the other a store of the dried heather used for bedding for livestock. Medd and Simms decided to sleep in this small building, although there was barely room for them both to bed down in. The weather closed in for the next three days and they spent most of that time burrowed under a few feet of dried heather in their tiny Capanna, desperately trying to keep warm on that exposed ridgeline.

George, my sister Yvonne's sweetheart, took it upon himself to befriend and care for the two men over the next week. Usually accompanied by his pal Bruno, he would carry supplies of basic food such as rice, potatoes, milk and bread up to the hut and then sit and chat with the men. They all enjoyed chatting about far-off peacetime London. Before the war George, born in London, had been a student at Pisa University, with hopes of studying medicine before being caught up in the pre-war exodus of Italian families back to their homeland.

George informed the Englishmen that the group of men they'd encountered when they had first got to the village were indeed deserters from the Italian Army that were in the same situation as he was. They were desperately avoiding been drafted by the German Army, so they were hiding here in the hills. They worked the land with sentries posted on all the tracks to warn of any approaching patrols. George told Medd and Simms that he would ensure they were also warned, should any Germans be sighted nearby. This relieved their anxiety, as they still felt very vulnerable in the location in which they were hiding.

Over the next few days, the small hut was made more habitable and waterproof by patching the walls and roof with clumps of moss. George was also able to supply them with another comfort from home – my sister Lillian always loved reading *Life* magazine and had brought many old copies with her from London. George grabbed a pile of these from our house and took them up to the hut. The two soldiers were delighted to pass the time reading through articles about a normal, peacetime world that now seem so far away for all of us.

So they spent the next week or so in the same way many hundreds of escaping British POWs were at that time in our region. After nights spent sheltering from the heavy autumnal rains, they would spend the days scavenging for firewood and any wild foodstuffs, such as mushrooms, whilst trying to avoid contact with the local population – aware that only one of the Italians that saw them needed to be sympathetic to the German cause for their location to be betrayed.

Peter Medd's hip injury improved and, as he became more mobile, he started to grow impatient and was soon talking to George of moving on. Bruno and George were enjoying the excitement of sheltering the British servicemen and tried to encourage them to stay for the winter in a larger more comfortable hut lower down in the valley, which was owned by Bruno's uncle. But the two Englishmen were wary of staying in the countryside where they so obviously stood out from the locals, and decided they would be on their way as soon as they could get updated news on the location of the advancing friendly forces.

As previously mentioned, there were many British servicemen trying to evade capture in our region at that time. A further excerpt from their book *The Long Walk Home* describes the experience of a fellow escapee along with their friendship with George's Uncle Palmiro, another local character. It also tells of an evening that Medd and Simms spent in my family's home which confirmed their decision to continue southwards.

For their own safety, the two British servicemen were hiding in the small hut a good distance from our village and high up on one of the ridges that overlooked Roggio and the surrounding valley. They had expressed the wish to George to come down to our house and listen to the radio in order to determine how far down the boot of Italy the Allied forces were.

Our house at the time was the only one with a radio in Roggio; listening to British broadcasts was absolutely forbidden so for my family to do this together with two escaped British officers was indeed very risky. However this is in fact just what we did.

So it was that George, my sister Yvonne's fiancé, was detailed one night to collect Peter Medd and Franks Simms and guide them surreptitiously to our house. Great care had to be exercised in those days as no one could be sure of who could be trusted, so George took great care in guiding them into the house without anyone in the village seeing them.

I remember Mum, Dad and my three sisters were quite excited at the prospect of entertaining two British officers in our home, despite the obvious risks. The air was filled with great anticipation: despite having lived in England for a long period of time my family would not have had occasion to associate with two such gentlemen due to our cultural diversity.

In the event, when George and the two boys arrived we were all to sit around our huge kitchen fire and enjoy a very full evening. Being of a very young age I would obviously take very little part in the general socialising and would merely be a very curious onlooker. Despite this, I have retained the events of that evening in my memory, due to my own recollections and the many times I have revisited the past with my sisters during family gatherings. Reading extracts from *The Long Walk Home* has also give me a glimpse of the mindset of our two guests that evening. My mother, despite our limited resources, was able to provide a suitable meal for which I am sure Peter and Frank were most appreciative. Thereafter they engaged in long reminiscences with George and my family about life and times in far away England. I know that British folk are considered to be far less emotional than their Latin counterparts and the stiff upper lip maxim must at all times be observed. However, on this occasion I am absolutely sure that these two young officers must have experienced deep emotions at being able to partake in a warm family atmosphere once more after such a long absence from their own families back home in Blighty.

The object of this visit was also to gather news from the radio and eventually, together with my father who had always been an avid radio listener, Peter and Frank would manage to tune in to British BBC broadcasts. Unfortunately they were to discover that Allied forces were still very far away from their present position. It seems that following this news they decided that, despite all the unforeseen difficulties, they must continue their journey in the endeavour to reach Allied lines. The Allies had landed on the southern tip of mainland Italy three weeks previously and had started the steady advance up the Italian peninsula.

So the very pleasant evening would eventually reach a conclusion and once more the reality of the moment had to be addressed. George would have had the task of guiding them back to the hideout, but instead of the distant refuge further up the mountain they would spend the night in a nearby empty barn and the journey back to their own hideout could be undertaken early the next morning.

It may sound implausible that one could roam around during the night without artificial light of any kind, but on a moonlit night visibility was remarkably good in our mountains. I remember making the same trip myself on a couple of occasions with food wrapped in a tea towel, which my mother had prepared for the British boys.

As my mind wanders back to those distant memories, the emotions that I felt are rekindled and, as then, I experience a sense of tempered excitement as I relive the trip I made from our house to the hideaway of Peter Medd and Frank Simms. This lay almost at the summit of Santa Cristina, an imposing mass which rises from the front of our village of Roggio.

It is difficult to describe this experience: recalling such a trip invites a cold shudder and almost incredulity that it did happen – a moonlit night with the heavens awash with stars high in those beautiful mountains of Garfagnana. I would make my way along a narrow path in the stillness of the night, the only sound I had for company was that of my own muted footsteps and the barely discernible distant gurgle of cascading water of a solitary mountain stream. This was in stark contrast to the daytime sound of birdsong, the constant din of sheep and cowbells and the reverberating sounds of woodcutters in the surrounding forests.

Alas, the Abrami's heroic support of Allied POWs eventually brought the inevitable betrayal. In his book Frank Abrami tells the story of his family's trials after my father and Peter Medd left them. The family continued to give help to escaping prisoners. On a fateful day in January 1945 when my father and Peter were safely back in England the Germans surrounded the village of Roggio blocking every exit. Soldiers burst into the Abrami house and dragged Frank's parents from the house. He too was pulled out of bed at gunpoint and made to show them the rest of the house.

His parents were taken on a forced march with other families under suspicion – the more unbearable as the Allied forces were just fifteen kilometres south of Roggio. Allied planes flew over frequently and suddenly a cluster of Allied planes spotted the column and swooped down menacingly. Panic set in, their captors scattered and they had a brief opportunity to escape. But then they reasoned – if they escaped the Germans would simply return and take the children as hostages. So they rejoined the column. A few kilometres further on the Allied planes appeared again causing renewed pandemonium.

This time they took refuge in a house. Was this divine providence, again? This time they decided to escape. After a horrific mountain crossing through the snow they reached Allied lines. As they spoke English and were both professional cooks they were given work in a British HQ and Frank's father was immediately given a British uniform. But it was a long time before they had news of their children, and vice versa.

No less agonising was the fate of others who had helped feed and shelter my father and Peter Medd. George (Giorgio

Ferrari known as George as he was born in London) sweetheart of Frank Abrami's youngest sister Yvonne, was arrested, escaped, then recaptured and shot by firing squad. Bruno, son of an English Cockney mother and a pro-Fascist father, joined the local partisans and died fighting in a skirmish in the hills above his home village. Both young men are buried in Roggio cemetery. All this is told in Frank Abrami's book.

*

Following their stay in Roggio the narrative continues in *The Long Walk Home*, my father taking over from Peter Medd on Day 28. My father's debriefing report, quoted earlier, also contains a description of their brief recapture as they neared Allied Lines.

> One foggy morning near Palena, we saw three men with mules, who looked like civilians, we asked them the way. One of them turned out to be a German soldier, dressed as an Italian except for his hat, the other two were Italian prisoners. He produced a revolver and asked us for our papers. Finding we had none, he told us to fall in with the other two, this we did, but after a few minutes ran for it. The German fired three shots and threw a grenade at us, but all missed.

The narrative of *The Long Walk Home* ends abruptly. My father and Peter Medd met the advancing British troops in the village of Lucito, in the modern region of Molise south of Abruzzo (which it was formerly part of) and north of Naples. My father wrote: 'The holiday was over. That evening we were in battledress.' However as he told the story to my mother there was an extra flourish. They first had to be held for debriefing to make sure that they were indeed British soldiers not German plants. He was placed in a pen and was desperate for a glass of water. He noticed the guard was in the uniform of the Sudan Defence Force with which he had served in the 1930s. He spoke to the guard in Arabic and the guard was so startled and thrilled to be addressed in his own language that he immediately brought my father a small banquet of food.

My father arrived back in England on December 26th, 1943. Soon after he married my mother and I was born nine months later on September 21st, 1944. By that time he was already in Palestine. My mother kept an air letter posted on June 27th from the Middle East Staff College. He wrote 'arrived today the last bit was the most trying as porters seem non-existent in ME and I have had to lug and tug boxes and things from one continent into another.'

His service in Palestine led him to write a novel (unpublished) about a sergeant who falls in love with a Palestine Christian girl in the aftermath of war. He deserts the army to help her and her family to organise resistance to the Jewish onslaught which was overrunning village after village in the battle to create a new Jewish state. The sergeant fights a tragic losing battle and eventually decides he must return to his regiment and face the inevitable court martial and prison sentence that will allow him to marry his sweetheart. All this is set against the background of the blowing up of the King David Hotel in Jerusalem in 1946, when many British officers were killed and many soldiers wondered where their loyalties lay as they were trapped between warring sides.

My father returned unexpectedly to Britain in 1945. This is evident from a letter he wrote to Harry Chard (supplied to me by Ian). It is addressed to Trooper Harry Chard in Bristol and written from the Combined Training Centre, Inveraray, Argyll on May 22nd (a fortnight after VE day).

Dear Chard,
I was brought back rather to my surprise to do a course in this country so I got your telegram a few

days ago. It is grand to think you are home again and I hope your brother from India was there to see you before he went back.

I gather from the date his leave was up that he would have been. It must have been a terrible shock to you to find all your family had died on your return and I sympathise deeply with you. I have to go to Bideford for a few days on this course and though I am rather hazy about distances I wonder if there is some place we could meet for lunch halfway between there and Bristol. You were a busman so you ought to know. I think I told you that it wasn't till I got back at the end of '43 that I found out you were still alive and that you had not been drowned between Tripoli and Naples...

In 1945 my father was promoted Lieutenant Colonel and in February 1946 was appointed Commanding Officer of the 8th Battalion of his regiment. A year later he was off to Ethiopia as General Staff Officer to the British Military Mission in Ethiopia.

In 1948, he was appointed Information Advisor to the British Military Mission in Greece. All I have of this episode is a phrase of my mother's in a letter to Lofty of July 13 1985 relating that he 'rounded up bandits in Greece.' In 1948 he was back in England with his Regiment and in 1950 posted to the Midland Brigade Training Centre. This coincides with my memory of last seeing him when I was six. In June 1951 he was off abroad again, arriving in Ankara to become Assistant Military Attaché.

Just over a year later, on September 3rd 1952, he was killed in a motor accident at Devrek, north of Ankara. My cousins believed that my father had been assassinated in a staged road accident. At the time this was a Soviet speciality, as chemical attacks are today. Turkey had recently joined NATO. This was the height of the Cold War – the Korean War had begun in 1950.

Another story came via John Hood, who had provided my mother with the description of life in the Sudan Defence Force in the 1930s. It came in a letter signed Dick (no surname), dated January 11th 1992 from Lower Tadhay, Hawkchurch, Axminster, Devon EX13 5UB. Dick's source was an acquaintance 'who in the '50s had served in Southern Command. He is an ex Territorial Army officer ... who transferred to the Pays Corps.'

There he met an 'RASC Staff Sergeant who had been Frankie's S/Sgt in Turkey and had been in the vehicle when they crashed'. The sergeant's story was that:

> They were asked to do a recce and roads reports in a certain mountainous area towards the Soviet border in NE Turkey – exactly where I don't know, though it was reported to be a bandit area. They had been warned by villagers of the danger from anti-foreign elements but pressed on. After passing through one rather hostile village, two or three wild dogs chased their vehicle and jumped into the back and attacked them. In trying to fend them off they lost control and went over the mountainside. Both men were badly injured. The S/Sgt came to and saw Frankie was still alive. He then passed out and when he came to Frankie was dead. The S/Sgt apparently was convinced that someone had visited the wreck and murdered Frankie. There was no explanation why the S/Sgt wasn't similarly dealt with.

John Hood tried to substantiate the story further but without success.

Several years later I was advised to write to the MoD asking for the report of the inquiry after my father's death – a standard procedure when a serving officer was killed. The reply came from the Army Historical Branch, Ministry of Defence, dated January 27th, 1999. It explained:

The Court of Enquiry does not contain the details you have requested, mainly being concerned with the actions which were taken after the accident occurred. However, on the 8th September 1952 the Military Attaché, Ankara, reported on the circumstances surrounding your father's death on the 3rd September and his subsequent funeral in the Crimean Cemetery, Istanbul on 5th September. The following is a transcript of part of the report.

Lt Col Simms was carrying out a short tour of the roads near the Black Sea coast and on the day in question was returning… to Ankara, accompanied by a non-commissioned officer of the British Training Staff, whom he had taken with him as a mechanic. At about 11.20 Lt Col Simms was driving along a stretch of road some 26 kilometres south of Devrek. The road here is tortuous and pursues an extremely winding course overlooking the bed of a stream. It appears that on rounding one of these corners the jeep was confronted with a truck belonging to the Highways Department and proceeding in the opposite direction. While negotiating his way past this truck, Lt Col Simms appears to have struck the left mudguard of the truck a glancing blow with the left side of his jeep, the blow being sufficient to force the front wheels of the jeep sharply to the right so that it left the road and plunged down an almost vertical drop of 60 or 70 ft to the bed of the stream below. Lt Col Simms received such internal injuries and damage to his legs that he died very shortly afterwards without regaining consciousness.

At approximately midnight on 3rd–4th September a party from the Embassy arrived at the place of the accident. Lt Col Simms body had not been removed from the ravine but had been left under guard in the shade until

Embassy representatives arrived. Some dozen gendarmes with the utmost care and with considerable difficulty then succeeded by the light of the full moon in getting the body up to the road whence it was taken in a truck to the nearest gendarme post and there properly attended to. Lt Col Simms's body was then taken to Istanbul arriving at approximately 19.30 hours on the evening of 4th September. The funeral took place at 10.00 hours on 5th September in the Crimean Cemetery… In addition to Their Excellencies the British Ambassador and Lady Helm, the mourners included a Turkish Colonel representing the Chief of the General Staff and a Commander of the First Army, British Service Attachés, Service Attachés of Canada, Pakistan, India, the United States, Italy France and Egypt (several of whom had travelled specially for the funeral from Ankara) members of the British Embassy, of the British Consulate General, Istanbul, and officers and men of the British Training Staffs. The pallbearers were British warrant and non-commissioned officers. A firing party of Turkish soldiers, provided by the Commander of the First Army, fired a final salute of five volleys over the grave at the end of the service. There were a very large number of wreaths, including some from all branches of the Turkish Armed Forces.

The news of my father's death was reported briefly in *The Times*. Three letters of condolence survive, sent to my mother by my father's sister. The first dated September 5th is from the Ambassador to my grandmother:

This morning we laid Frank to rest in the lovely Crimean cemetery overlooking the sea – a beautiful, peaceful spot shaded by large trees. There was a Turkish firing party and his colleagues were there, many of them having come down from Ankara overnight. It was all very moving and now his grave is covered with masses of lovely flowers.

The second, dated the next day September 6th, was from Major-General A. C. Shortt, CB, OBE, Director of Military Intelligence at the War Office:

> While working for us, Lieut. Colonel Simms had shown himself to be most conscientious and energetic and his work has been of great value. Moreover, he possessed great charm of manner, and I know that his loss will be most deeply felt both in his Regiment and amongst those who have been working with him more recently.

The third, most impressively, was on headed paper from the beautiful 17th-century Chateau de Courances on the edge of the Forest of Fontainebleau. It runs:

From: Field Marshal the Viscount Montgomery of Alamein KG, GCB, DSO
10 September 1952

Dear Mrs Simms
I would like to tell you how sorry I was to hear of the death of your son in Turkey. I, of course, knew him well as I am colonel of the Royal Warwickshire Regt. I was probably the last officer of the Regiment to see him as I was in Ankara in May last and met him at the British Embassy. I am going to Turkey again on Saturday next and will doubtless learn some further details. On behalf of the Regiment I send you our deep sympathy.

Yours sincerely
Montgomery of Alamein

*

Thanks to the recollections and researches of those I have quoted so extensively in this memoir I have learnt a huge amount about the father I barely knew, who had been killed shortly before my eighth birthday, and who I rarely saw as he was away so much on active service.

General David Lloyd-Owen, who I quoted earlier, described my father as appearing not to know 'the meaning of fear'. Lofty Carr elaborates on this in a letter to my mother:

> He taught me a lot about controlling my fears. In my opinion he was not 'fearless' he was courageous, he could conceal his fears. After an initial period of exposure to his terrifying methods (during which I, personally, was demoralised) one began to rebuild oneself on lines more appropriate to anyone accompanying him on his exploits. I suppose that since he chose to cart me around with him I may not have been as inadequate as I often felt.

Lofty added that my father:

> Had a great sense of fun and always made sure he paid back for any pranks we played on him. When we first met him we had to go through a gap in Mussolini's barbed wire separating Egypt from Libya. I jokingly said to him 'The officer always goes first.' (It was a routine trip). He duly went through but a few days later when we were firing mortar bombs for practice one failed to go off. I think now that he had doctored it. To scare the daylights out of me he said 'Come on Carr, we'll go and see why it didn't explode'. We went up to it and he gave the thing a good kick.

I began writing this afterword with little more than family memories. But in the course of six months, following an initial approach from Andrew Adams, I have found windows into many different aspects and periods of my father's life and service, though some months and years remain a mystery. I have found so much, in particular from Lofty Carr, Ian Chard, the Long Range Desert Group Association and the Abrami family - Frank, Mario and their families. In addition I would like to thank Charles Woodrow for his help on army matters. I am also grateful to my cousins Blake Simms, Naomi Tucker and Jane Goman and her husband John, and to my wife Anne and sons Francis and Christopher who have spurred me on. I am naturally keen to find more and any leads will be gratefully received.

*Marcus Binney*
*Jersey 2019*

## NOTE

After my father was killed in 1952 my mother remarried, three years later, another war hero, Sir George Binney DSO, who had carried off what Hugh Dalton, the Government Minister responsible for SOE, Churchill's Special Operations Executive, described as the first great success of the secret war.

In a daring escapade in January 1941 my stepfather brought five unarmed merchant ships through the German blockade of the Skaggerak – avoiding minefields, the Luftwaffe and the German naval vessels that were waiting for them. The cargo was 26,000 tons of ball bearings, special steels and equipment vital for aircraft and tank manufacture. It was a full year's supply of essential materials which could not be obtained from any other source including the USA.

My stepfather adopted me and I have his name. I grew up on more war stories. His ambition in his later years was to write up his war exploits – for which he received both a knighthood in the Prime Minster's honours and later a DSO. However he never completed them and it fell to me to help commission Ralph Barker to write *The Blockade Busters* (Chatto & Windus 1976).

All these thrilling war stories led me to embark on a book about the war *The Women who Lived for Danger*. When this was published the Foreign Office contacted me to say they had a cache of secret papers on my step-father's second operation, which I used in a chapter in my book *Secret War Heroes*. More recently his exploits have been revisited in *SOE's Balls of Steel* (The History Press 2013) by Sophie Jackson, on Operation Rubble.

# A NOTE ON THE VILLAGE OF SILLICO AND THE CHARACTERS WHO HELPED MEDD & SIMMS

> This place, we felt, was safe enough, for no road reached
> it, only muletracks twisting down into the green
> desolate valley.

SILLICO, pictured on the cover of this edition, was remote and extremely parochial, but like many of the mountain villages it was linked by emigration to the wider complex world. Two figures flit across Medd's stage in his telling of the brief stay there after leaving Roggio, bit players in his drama but of central significance to the conflicted local history of Resistance and Civil War.

> The village priest arrived. He was the real organiser
> behind this help to escaped prisoners in Sillico.

Don Guiglemo Sessi, a native of Massa Carrera beyond the mountains, for the whole of his life the priest of this hamlet of 300 souls and its tiny neighbour Capraia, was thirty-six in 1943 and already ten years a priest to the shepherds, sharecroppers and few landowners of his parish. A cultured man who took a degree in literature from Pisa University and knew the intellectuals of Lucca, he was also a stubborn orthodox Catholic and an ideological monarchist who nevertheless had little time for the present King. Neither openly for nor against the Fascist regime, when it fell he followed the dictates of his faith and stood with the persecuted and the refugees: sheltering Jews, political dissidents and Allied escapers. Don Sessi's choice would cost him ecclesiastical preferment after the war, when he refused his Bishop's request to testify in favour of the Fascist governor of Lucca at the latter's trial.

Two months after Simms and Medd had passed through Sillico, Don Sessi was arrested for helping escapers but was released on the intercession of senior Churchmen. He returned immediately to his old activities and in 1944 developed close contacts with one of the famous partisan commanders, 'Pippo' Ducchesi, to the extent that a German patrol called on the priest to ensure their safe passage up and down the mountain.

His luck nearly ran out in early 1945 when a Fascist-German patrol arrived to arrest him. Such an order in the febrile closing days of Fascism in Italy could well have meant death. Hostages were being taken and shot in reprisal for partisan attacks.

He convinced the German soldier detailed to escort him that he had to collect a stout pair of shoes from the presbytery. The German must have been either very well disposed or very dozy. Telling the soldier to wait in the main room, Don Sessi went into the kitchen, from there to the church, from the church to the street and to the woods. A day later he crossed the frontlines to safety.

\*

About nine o'clock, while we were digesting our supper over the kitchen fire, our good lady's husband walked in. He was in business in Lucca… He was a typical Fascist, the hard bony face, the sleek black hair, the smooth blue suit with overpadded shoulders. We recognised him at once for one of those cold ruthless types whose object was to keep in well with both sides and swim with whatever current caught him.

Mario Bianchi was indeed a Fascist, and in 1944, despite already having helped many escapers, would join the 'Black Brigade' (Brigada Nera) of Fascist volunteers formed to fight the partisans. His name is bound up with the atrocity at Castelnuovo di Garfagnana, some 8 miles to the west of Sillico, of September 23rd 1944, when a party of Brigada Nera, high on alcohol and fear, took revenge on innocent bystanders for a botched partisan attack on their billets which had wounded seven. Eight civilians were taken by the Fascists from their daily work and summarily shot down.

Bianchi was known in Sillico as a mild man. Eyewitnesses to one of the murders on the September 23rd described him as refusing to join in shooting at a corpse and there is no account of him taking part in the killings. He was nevertheless a volunteer member of Brigada Nera and he was there. This was enough to seal his fate.

Against this familiar black and white stereotype must be set his standing in Sillico and Capraia where, a graduate teacher with some knowledge of medicine, he was known for his readiness to go out of his way in time and money to help fellow villagers and to be someone who 'would not hurt a fly'. His loyalty to his village seems to have been unquestionable, his practical help to Allied escapers demonstrable – how harsh is Medd's judgement of him?

Towards the end of 1943 Bianchi had his house by one account 'full of English' and denounced the German reward offered for turning escaped POWs in. A veteran of the Fascist March on Rome, he was nevertheless arrested and interrogated. When released, he opened his house again to escapers and yet, as we see above, he was present at the murders at Castelnuovo.

Immediately at the end of the war he was required, as an ex-Fascist, to report for compulsory reconstruction work. He was abducted from that work by 'persons unknown' and never seen again.

Like several others, his body lies undiscovered to this day in the chestnut woods of the mountains, mute testimony to the trauma that did not stop with peace.

*Andrew Adams*
*April 2019*

# THE PADULA TUNNEL

CAMPO 35 was probably the most beautiful prisoner of war camp in Europe. We were accommodated in what in mediaeval times had been the Carthusian Monastery of St. Lawrence called then the Kingdom of Silence.

It was set in a fruitful and shining valley surrounded by mountains some eighty miles south-east of Salerno. It was a large building with honey-coloured walls and roofs of old and lichened tiles; in honour of its patron saint, the building was shaped like a gridiron.

The main courtyard round which we lived was covered with grass and surrounded by a lofty colonnade under which it was possible to walk, however bad the weather. Opening off the colonnade were some twenty-four suites of rooms. These were all of the same design and consisted of a small entrance lobby with a passage leading to a verandah and a small walled garden and a door with a bricked-up passage that led to two empty rooms upstairs. There were two large rooms on the ground floor with big windows overlooking the garden and the mountains beyond the valley. There was also a narrow passage some twelve yards long ending in a small window and a lavatory opening off it at the end. These passages formed the arms of the gridiron and also the walls which divided the gardens. These gardens were only overlooked by the quarters to which they belonged. Bounded on either side by these passages they were closed at the end by a wall about six feet high which ran the length of the building. Most of the gardens had roses, lilac and a few peach or plum trees. They were regarded as the private property of those who lived in the rooms to which they belonged. Their owners could augment the meagre Italian rations by growing potatoes, tomatoes or sweetcorn.

Beyond the wall at the end of the garden and out of sight was the wire, and guarding it were sentries who sang endless snatches of opera through their noses. Beyond this again was a very large field some 200 acres in extent surrounded by a wall 15 feet high. Life in these quarters was not uncomfortable. We had good spring beds, sheets and the camp sustained a flourishing black market from which we were able to buy butter, cheese, huge iced cakes, eggs by the dozen and petrol tins of home-made cherry jam. Richard Carr who had been in the Long Range Desert Group with me also kept chickens. Upstairs above the colonnade was a long passage which housed the subalterns in considerably more discomfort than we captains enjoyed below. They had no privacy, while we were able to keep one of our rooms as a sitting room by overcrowding the other with beds. They had no fruit trees, no garden and no view. They shared with us the seven-acre football field and the grass-covered courtyard, the spacious panelled dining hall which had a fascinating picture of the *Miracle of Cana* at one end, showing the feast with the peasants all dressed up in cloth of gold and pearls, and in one corner a macaw on a perch.

Padula in fact, especially for those who lived below, had a great deal to be said for it. It had beauty, dignity, serenity and a lovely climate, sufficient food, and nights loud with the song of nightingales and no responsibility.

Richard and I made our first attempt at tunnelling with knives up an extremely hard and narrow passage we excavated under the stairs leading to the garden. We hoped to get into the cellars which we knew existed below our quarters; we could see their blocked-up windows above the flower beds. However, we reached a large solid mediaeval wall the penetration of which was beyond our tools and our inclination. It was so narrow that we had to wriggle forward with our arms in front of us and pick at the mortar lying on the hard and rough stone floor with the equally hard and pointed stone roof two inches above our heads.

We then decided to escape by the roof. This involved a lot of climbing over very loose and easily cracked tiles. Our progress at night when we were on a reconnaissance seemed to us to be marked by a series of cracks like pistol shots; however, having negotiated one long steep roof and started on the next, we found ourselves close to a hitherto unexpected sentry. The exits off the roof over the Italian quarters were heavily wired and we had to descend the roof getting caught in the searchlight for an agonising moment. At this period Richard and I thought we would escape fairly soon and as a guide to how lavishly this camp was provisioned by the black market, we hard boiled three dozen eggs between us, thinking wrongly that hard-boiled eggs would keep longer than fresh ones. This proved a fallacy and when we went to eat them they were all bad and had to be buried in the garden.

One day three of the officers from upstairs, Alan Hurst Brown, Rifle Brigade, Roy Howard, King's Dragoon Guards, and Peter Bateman, R.N., came to see us to ask if they could start a tunnel from our room. The Italians had only allowed us the use of the gardens on condition they were not used for escaping, an assurance which had been given by the senior British officer. The doors leading to the verandahs and the gardens had been bricked up when we arrived. We showed them our first effort and worked a few days at that and then gave it up again. We promised them however that if we ever did start a tunnel from Room 6 we would let them in on it. It was obvious that if one could get into the cellars it would be easy to tunnel but the floors were very thick and made of centuries-old concrete and we felt it would be hard to get through, and harder still to hide. In addition, a tunnel would only bring one out in the large field behind the sentries which seemed to be lying fallow that year. It was a very big field and there seemed little object in coming up twenty yards from the sentry with no cover at all.

The summer went on and someone in the village denounced the black market and it suddenly came to an end and the Commandant got the sack. But by now we were getting Red Cross parcels regularly so its loss was not noticed.

One evening towards the end of July, Richard, Tom Murdoch of the Wiltshire Yeomanry and myself were walking round the playing field, the western side of which gave one a view towards the outer wall past our room and a glimpse of the field, and we saw the Italians were planting maize there. We did not know how long maize took to grow, but we did realise that such a tall and rustling crop would be ideal for making a break.

We went straight to our room. Richard pointed out the place we were to start work; as one stepped from the end of the passage into the lavatory there was an irregular shaped patch of bricks about two feet square, the only bricks in the concrete floors of our quarters. The lavatory itself was built over the corner of the garden where in the old days it had emptied. I went upstairs and asked Jack Green, a Sapper lieutenant and one of the few remaining pupils of my Arabic class, to come down on a matter of some importance. He came at once. I was standing beneath the tree picking plums in that garden when he came. He fell for the bait of ripe fruit as an ancestor of his had once fallen in another garden. To us the removal of the bricks seemed difficult, and we thought it would be impossible to ever put them back so that they would escape notice. Jack, however, was full of ideas. He went next door to Room 5 where the officer who mended the chairs was allowed some tools and borrowed a saw. We soon had the bricks up and found they barred an old trapdoor leading through a vaulted roof to the cellar. The first thing to do though was to put the bricks back. Jack quickly cut a table top into the shape of the hole and cemented the bricks on to it. String from Red Cross parcels was nailed on to form handles and pushed into the cracks which were then carefully filled with dust. It looked as good as ever. String, like the mortar, had to be stolen from the Italians. But Tony Hay, who had also been in the Long Range Desert Group with Richard and I, had a flair for stealing, surprising in a Guards officer. That night in Room 6 we had a long discussion and we found that everyone in the room was not prepared to work on the tunnel nor to escape by it if it was successful. This was very typical of the attitude towards escape at Padula. There were four of us, Richard Carr, Tom Murdoch, Tony Hay and myself; then also from Room 6 we recruited John Greenwood, 9th Lancers, and Brian Smith of the Fleet Air Arm, and from upstairs we had the three subalterns who had approached us before and Jack Ling of the Rifle Brigade, who had been coming over the roofs with Richard and I, and Jack Green the Sapper.

The next day we started removing the trapdoor and clearing the trap itself of blocks of marble which we put in the garden; we had with the aid of Tony Hay's string made a rope ladder and I dropped on to the floor of the cellar. It had a cement floor and ran the whole length of the passage from our room to the lavatory. It was illuminated slightly by cracks in the bricked-up windows half below ground looking on to the garden, and by cracks in a blocked-up doorway opening towards the wire which was some six feet beyond it. From the garden we had taken some large iron spikes which held the climbing roses in position. We started to scrape a hole through the concrete. It was hard going and by the end of the first day we had excavated a hole about four inches across for the concrete was about three inches thick; below it was earth. I had succeeded in secreting during the six months of my captivity an escaping file which I had kept in the pleat of my battle dress blouse pocket. Whenever the Germans or Italians had searched me, I had helpfully removed my keys which were worn on a lanyard from this pocket and they had investigated no further. We now used it to cut an iron bedstead in half and bound it together to make a more stable and hard-wearing ladder than the rope one which we had used hitherto. The tunnel had really started now and it was August 1st.

The next day we were still picking at the concrete when Tom Murdoch had an idea that if we made a great deal of noise no sentry would suspect it of being caused by people with anything to hide. We went out into the garden and fetched in a marble block and got it through the trap into the cellar. We then scraped the earth away from under the hole we had already made so laboriously and then brought the marble block crashing down on the unsupported lip. The noise this made reverberated in the barrel-vaulted cellar but the nearest sentries who were distant some 15 and 30 yards respectively paid no attention. Tom had been right. In three hours we had broken the concrete for an area of about 12 feet by 4 feet. In taking this and other risks we were acting on the assumption that if our tunnel was not finished before the maize was cut it would be useless.

That day we had another stroke of luck. We found amongst some straw in the cellar two old spade heads. In addition to this, Tony Hay, who had permission to visit the Italian quarters to collect Red Cross parcels, had come back with a pick under his jacket.

At this time Roy Howard came to see me as the senior member of Room 6 and told me that the tunnel was the idea of his two companions and himself from upstairs and they demanded to be let in on it. We had always intended to let them in on it, but up to now there had not been sufficient work for eleven people. However, as a result of this disagreement, we allowed them to start work on condition they went out last. People living upstairs did not run the same risk of being sent to the punishment camp if the tunnel was found prematurely.

Having started, we worked hard and fast at the tunnel. We had two shifts of three hours each in the morning and two in the afternoon. We worked nearly twelve hours a day. Roll was called twice a day, once in the morning between 7.30 and 9.30 and again in the evening between 5.30 and 7.00. Fortunately the Italians were very slack about calling us in quickly and it was generally a quarter of an hour before everyone had got on parade, after the bugle had gone. This gave ample time for those at the face to come up, wash in the lavatory which was in the useful position of a pit head bath, while the others in the room put down the alarm bell, replaced the trap and stuffed the string in the cracks and swept the dust over it. Collecting the dust was a very boring job, sweeping it and then sifting it through a piece of gauze into a box. Many people, including myself, always evaded this work whenever possible, but Tony Hay went on doing it day after day in addition to his shifts at the tunnel and plaiting rope from stolen Red Cross parcel string at which he was extremely good.

The system we worked on was as follows. At the end of the passage in the outer wall was a small window rather high up which overlooked the maize; immediately below was a path never used, then the wire some six feet wide and then the sentries' beat. One of the officers in the room did quartermaster and below the window was a strong wooden rack which held clothing and gave No. 1 a secure seat to look through the window. The window itself was covered with fine gauze which was supplied by the Italians to keep flies out. It was impossible to see out if the window was shut owing to the thickness of the wall beyond the gauze. No. 1's job was to report the movement of the sentries who were stationed about 15 yards away on the left and 30 on the right and who were continually moving about to talk to each other. He gave three signals by means of a tin on a piece of string which hung from the rack by the trap door. These consisted of 'all clear' which meant both the sentries were at the far end of their beats and noise was no object. The second signal was 'work quietly.' This was used when both sentries were at their boxes and meant that the pick could not be used but work such as collecting earth in heaps by hand and putting it in the bucket could be carried on. The third signal was 'stop,' and was used whenever the sentries were standing opposite the room on the line of the tunnel and no one could move. The clump of the sentries' boots on the hard ground was generally audible some way off. But there were some orphan children who generally went barefooted, employed on the farm, who were a constant source of alarm to a drowsy No. 1 on a hot afternoon. Number 2 stood on the floor of the cellar and worked the pulley down the vertical shaft we had had to dig to get clear of the foundations. He emptied the buckets as they came up at the back of the cellar. For us fortunately there was no difficulty in disposing of the earth. The buckets we had also stolen from the Italians. As the tunnel grew longer No. 2 had to pump air to the face. He also had to repeat signals that came from the watcher at the window to No. 3. No. 3 sat at the bottom of the twelve-foot shaft on the bottom step, pulling on a rope from the darkness of the tunnel, and lurching down the wooden railway which Jack Green had made from sawn-up Italian tables, would come a sledge with a bucket full of earth on it. He would hook the bucket on the pulley for No. 2 to take and put back the empty one for No. 1. He would also repeat the signals. No. 1 worked at the face using the pick, a spade, a spike or his hands as the occasion demanded. He filled the buckets and signalled for them to be pulled back down the line.

It was a very efficient tunnel, having no difficulty in getting rid of the spoil. It was fairly big, about 3ft. by 2ft., and as it was so big we worked quickly, often doing a yard a day. The earth was heavy clay and needed no revetting at any point, though we had alarms when we were under the field which was flooded to irrigate the maize once a week and the water came in.

We had many alarms; too many people in the camp got to know about the tunnel, and the Italians had a special squad of 'tunnel diviners' as we called them who were continuously having snap searches. On several occasions we had to put the trap down in a hurry leaving the shift still below. Twice the Italians left a sentry in the passage and he had to be decoyed away to another room to enable the workmen to get up and get dressed in time for roll-call. Meanwhile those who were off duty had to get fit by physical exercises and walking for two hours or so round the playing field and there were other preparations to make. Clothes had to be procured. Some, like Tony and Tom, had blankets cut up to form jackets and caps. Some of the downstairs rooms had walnut trees and from them I scrounged sufficient to boil my battle dress trousers and to dye them a rich shade of chocolate. We also had maps to copy. Some prisoners had still managed to secrete the silk escaping maps with which they had been issued before capture. These were not a great deal of good as we were so far south in Italy that our camp did not appear. Neither did these maps mark railways, a serious omission. After I had copied my maps I hid them behind a loose stone in the garden wall. Here, some fortnight later, they were found by the tunnel divining squad and I was on the mat and sentenced to seven nights cells. This was an almost ideal punishment. After supper I walked through to the Italian guard room and was locked in for the night in a fairly large room with an excellent light for reading. I thus had the privileges of having a room to myself each night for a week and still worked on the tunnel in the daytime. The tunnel itself was proceeding well. The twelve-foot shaft which we estimated would bring us below the foundations did so exactly and was led into by a series of steps cut out of the cellar floor. The 'pulley' was arranged by a rope and a hook made out of two nails. The railway line which had to be lengthened almost daily was made by Jack Green and Brian Smith out of table tops; fortunately the Italians never checked up on accommodation stores. The electric light flex also had to be scrounged and lengthened fairly frequently. The tunnel became the guiding power of our lives. As soon as we saw that roll-call was to be late or was over early, the first shift would be down and would stay down for their three hours, perhaps fortified by a cup of tea being lowered to them. Except for closing the trap for luncheon and the evening roll-call it remained open, except for an alarm, all day. As the tunnel got longer it became necessary to have a pump, as the air got worse with each foot.

When we started work, two other tunnels were already going, one in the room next door and another several rooms away which was worked in fits and starts. The one in the room next door started from the garden through a buried box of plants. One day an Italian soldier kicked the edge of this box with his foot. He investigated, took away the earth, pulled up the box, and the shaft was in view. This discovery had several effects on us. Firstly, as there was electric light in this tunnel, the Italians switched it off during the day and we had to make a substitute with margarine lamps. Secondly, all hose which was owned by the owners of the gardens was confiscated and this meant that we would have to steal it back to make our pipe line for our pump. Thirdly, when people said, as they so often did, 'Is it true you've got a tunnel in Room 6?' we could no longer say, 'You must be thinking of the people next door, they're supposed to have one.' The Italians were naturally annoyed that the assurance about not using the gardens had been broken, and redoubled their efforts to find other tunnels.

Not only were the Italians on our trail, the morale at Campo 35 was very bad and most of the officers there were very much against people trying to escape, though there was a body which called itself the escape committee.

Two days before we decided to start our tunnel, Richard and I had been told by this committee that no one must try to escape for two months as the Italians had just promised to give us a daily wine ration which would be cut if any one tried to get away. Of the prisoners at Padula, 10 per cent I would say were actively prepared to escape by some exertion and risk on their own part, 20 per cent would talk continously about escaping but had no intention of doing anything about it. The remainder of the camp never intended to escape themselves and disliked the idea of others trying. I, meanwhile, was now classified by the Italians as 'Stulto'; they either classified those who were considered possible escapers as 'stupid' or 'dangerous'. I was annoyed to be down as 'stupid'. But it was not long before, thanks to the efforts of Richard and Tony and myself, the Long Range Desert Group was to be the only 100 per cent 'dangerous' unit in Italy's prison camps.

We had thus to circumvent several difficulties, though compared to what most tunnellers go through, they were I suppose very easy. To start with, the replacement of electricity by lamp was done by making a wick and putting it in a tin of margarine or solid brilliantine, but only certain kinds of the latter burnt. It was always a bitter moment having to part with margarine from one's Red Cross parcels to keep the lamp going when one's turn came.

The first time there was a roll-call after this new form of illumination, we washed as usual and then went on parade, not realising that the soot from the lamp had sooted up our nostrils and they were coal black. Fortunately we discovered this before the Italian officers came round and had time to remedy it.

The pump was becoming more and more of a necessity every day and was made by Brian Smith. It was a substantial wooden affair worked by No. 5 standing on the cellar floor holding it in position with his feet. It was about 3ft. high and for a washer two round pieces of leather were cut from a wind jerkin of mine. This pump also, like the new lamp, was an eater of margarine.

John Greenwood produced the hose back again. He summoned the sentry who now supervised the watering of the gardens which had to be done through the windows from the taps in the lavatories and took him into a quarter some distance away from ours. Here he diverted the sentry's attention, cut off half the hose pipe with a razor blade and wrapped it round himself. This was joined on to the previous piece we had saved when we had learnt that hoses were to be handed in to the Italians.

The difficulties with the guards became greater as time went on; they were more certain than ever that we had a tunnel in Room 6 and were searching for it almost every day. Their spirits were very high as they thought they would be in Alexandria shortly. The leading tunnel diviner was continuously coming in and often stood on the trapdoor and tapped it with a heavy iron staff and still failed to notice it, it was so well packed beneath. The bricks of the trap too often came away or got broken with the frequent lifting and had to be replaced. Italian mortar, unlike Roman, does not last very long. On one occasion the trap was dropped while being replaced and a lot of bricks broken. Jack Green, who was suffering from malaria at the time, had to leave his bed and come downstairs to remedy the situation.

There was a peculiarly unattractive Italian officer called Benincasa who was the leader of the 'taunt the British ' school. He bet me that the Italians (and the Germans) would be in Alexandria on September 1st. I said, 'Make it the 15th and I'll give you a bottle of Marsala.' He hesitated and I said, 'Make it the 20th.' He agreed to this bet which he made in front of several British officers and some Italian soldiers. Yet he refused to pay at the end and got abusive about it into the bargain.

One day Richard and I were sunbathing in the garden when Benincasa came in with three Italian soldiers armed with picks. Benincasa said, 'I am going to find your tunnel today,' and ordered the men to break down the bricked-up windows of the cellar. There was a shift in there at the time but their feelings can have been no worse than ours as we watched the soldiers swing their picks. We turned over unable to watch the end of all our hopes any further. They had only to let a very little light into the cellar to see how full of earth that cellar was. Three blows of the picks and they stopped, finding I suppose that we hadn't gone through that way.

Towards the end the strain became greater; we had to lie to outsiders – 'Held up by rock' – 'by subsidence,' so that as few as possible should know the day we intended to leave. The strain of the searches got worse and worse each time, we had done so much more work. This of course was not noticed by those who lived upstairs who missed the anxiety of the guards' nocturnal visits and did not have a garden or such comfortable quarters like ourselves to exchange for the damp cells of Camp 5 where all those who tried to escape were sent.

In the evenings we had continuous arguments about how far we had gone, and whether we were keeping the level. Tom Murdock produced a spirit level from a bottle and with Tony's string we would nightly measure up the tunnel. Except that most people had a slight tendency to pick to the right, we kept very straight and level.

We had a big stroke of luck going under the path which was the sentries' beat; it had seemed always a dangerous prospect. But that day a threshing machine was brought into the field some 200 yards away and the noise it made enabled us to get under and beyond the path during the one and a half days it was there. We were able to work flat out with the pick the whole time.

Our chief trouble was the slope in the ground; we could see from the window where No. 1 kept watch that the ground beyond the wire definitely sloped. But as we could only see it from above it was difficult to judge its angle and whether we were three feet or six from the surface. The time was now coming when we must let the escape committee see how far we had got. They came prepared to scoff at our efforts. But, after we had shown them the passage and told them to find the trap for themselves and they had failed, they became impressed. When they descended by the sawn-up bedstead and saw the pump, the pick, the railway line, the sledge with its ropes and buckets, and, above all, the size of the tunnel, they became, though they tried not to show it, annoyed. Some of them had tunnelled at Sulmona with table knives, crawling on their stomachs, and a donkey had walked over their tunnel so that it fell in. They regarded our working conditions as too luxurious. However, after having seen it, looked at our escape clothes and asked us about map and routes, they consented to give us a hundred lire note each for our journeys to Switzerland or Yugoslavia.

The Brigadier insisted that we should take with us two New Zealanders, John Redpath and Jim Craig, who had been taken recently in the Greek Islands arranging the escape of soldiers cut off there in 1941. We agreed on condition they went out last. John Redpath was a mining engineer and was of considerable value to us during the few days he worked in the tunnel.

We were now faced with the problem of surfacing and from our measurements we imagined we would come up some twenty yards beyond the sentries. We were handicapped by not knowing how far the surface was above our heads. This surfacing from below secretly was a problem beyond even John Redpath or Jack Green's experience. They started by revetting the tunnel for the first time and driving it upwards at an incline of thirty degrees. This was carried on for some twelve feet, revetting with chopped-up tables the whole way. A metal tube was then made with a stick in it which was pushed upward through the earth and the stick then pulled out. At once a cold gust of air swept through the tunnel and the green stalks of maize were visible. The news was brought to me on the verandah of the garden where I was holding an Arabic class. The lesson was cut short that very day.

Most of us had been preparing food in the form of chocolate, toffee and biscuits. The biscuits were made from the flour obtained by grinding those supplied by the Canadian

Red Cross and adding sugar, meat extract and rebaking them. Clothes which were difficult to hide in rooms were left in the cellar. But as this was damp and was not free from rats, we left our food elsewhere, particularly the large cheeses which we had saved from the days when the black market flourished. I have already said that above our rooms there were two others which were empty. Twin doors in the entrance lobby when opened revealed the bricked-up passage leading upstairs. We removed a large part of the bricks behind our door and left our food hanging up in the passage beyond. This half door was always left closed and the other half open, exposing the blocked-up passage. The guards naturally thought this ran behind both doors and never bothered to open the other half. I had got this idea from reading the story of the man who hid in the cupboard for four years in General Spear's book 'Liason 1914.'

The escape committee were now approached by some forty people who demanded the right to go out of our tunnel, the order of departure to be drawn for by lot. We refused to agree to this decision for which we were much criticised, pointing out that we had done all the work, run all the risk of being sent to the punishment camp, that if forty people got out they could never hope to hide such a large number and that the whole countryside would be roused. We said that the eleven of us and the two New Zealanders would go the first night and that the whole camp could go the second night as we would guarantee that the Italians would not be able to find either exit or entrance if they would stage our departure so that it did not look as if Room 6 was involved. They agreed to this.

The next day I was sitting in the garden when the tunnel diviner came in and said, 'I know you have a tunnel here and you had much better tell me where it is; you can never hope to hide it from us.' I looked up and I said as ingenuously as I could in Italian, 'I know, I would tell you if we had one because you are just like a great big wonderful hunting dog.' He took this as a great compliment and threw his chest out and purred with delight and went off without searching at all.

On the afternoon of September 12th we were all ready to go, although the escape committee said that if we didn't go that night we wouldn't be allowed to go at all as there were others being held up who wanted to escape by a different route. So that afternoon Tony Hay got busy enlarging the hole. We then drew lots. Tom Murdoch and Richard were to go first, then John Greenwood and Brian Smith, then Jack Ling and I, Jack Green and Tony Hay, Alan Hurst Brown, Roy Howard and Peter Bateman and then the two New Zealanders.

The method of covering up the escape was this: All the empty beds in Room 6 were to be filled by those willing to go the following night and the beds upstairs of those who had moved into our room were to be done with dummies. They were very ingeniously done by Tom Barker with the tufts of maize or dyed clippings off a sheepskin for hair and were most realistic.

The last afternoon a search party led by the tunnel diviner doubled into the courtyard and came straight into Room 6. We had barely time to get the trap down before they were there. They searched for some twenty minutes and went out. We were glad it was the last day.

That evening after supper we came back into Room 6 some of us early; there were three sittings for meals and half of us had changed over to first sitting so that work could go on without a break throughout the day. As the room filled up it became very crowded and very gay. At 9 o'clock we were not allowed to leave our rooms and we therefore very anxious when two Italian soldiers came into the lobby and went straight into the garden. If they had come into the room the game would have been up, for some of us were in our 'civilian' clothes and all those who were to sleep in our beds were present which made the room very crowded.

It was a very excited party as we got down through the trap for the last time in the order we had drawn and sat in the dark tunnel.

The tunnel was some sixty feet long and had taken us six weeks to build!

I had got the occupants of the rooms on either side to play sentimental Italian songs on the gramophone to drive the sentries from their posts. After we were all out, Garry Cole was going to cement the trap into position and we had nothing to do but wait until it was our turn to go out. It was very black in the tunnel and it took a long time for Richard Carr was very stout and took the best part of three-quarters of an hour to get out, the reverberation of his heels on the floor making us certain that all was lost. It was a difficult exit, first of all on one's back for the twelve feet of the incline, then one had to put one's arms up through the hole whose sides mercifully stayed firm and without a foot rest pull oneself up, equipment and all, it required a hard physical effort. Someone early on had left a water bottle in the tunnel and every one who crawled over it seemed to kick it. Sitting in the dark I heard Tony say to Jack Green 'we'll never get out with Frank making so much noise.' He was disappointed when I told him it was still Richard trying to get out and that he had a long time to wait yet.

At last it was my turn, I put my haversack up on the ground and pulled myself out gasping. I was looking through the maize stalks at the arc lamp lit wall and the windows, at the wire and the sentries' feet, which was not as far as we had expected, only some ten feet away. While I lay there struggling to get my breath back, a sentry came down and stopped right opposite me for what seemed an age. I was terrified that Jack Green would try to come out after me. Fortunately someone peering through the window where No.1 had so often watched had seen him and had sent down word. When he was gone I crawled off through the maize which dry and tall now rustled continuously in the slightest breeze, carrying my haversack in my mouth.

After some two hundred yards of this I started to walk and soon made my way to the corner of the fifteen foot wall where the others would be. Richard and Tom had taken a rope ladder with them. Richard and Jack Ling were there, John and Brian had gone. I suggested to Richard that he should join us as Tom had not yet shown up. Richard decided to wait for Tom who appeared shortly after we had left. We were soon up the wall with a heave from Richard and dropped down into the road. We decided to turn south and work round the back of the village.

Just after we struck the road the monastery clock struck twelve. It was the September 13th, my brother's birthday. There was another omen that night, for the moon was the Moon of Ramadan, four weeks fasting and four days feasting. Neither of them worked.

Jack and I soon ran into some very thick bramble-filled thickets and decided to turn back north, skirting the outer wall of the monastery garden as we went. We passed some farms where a dog barked and began to climb a very stony mountain, here we met Brian Smith. Our plan was to make for the East Coast and then climb on a goods train to the frontier. It was a long way from Padula, south east of Salerno to the Swiss border. Brian was going north so we parted.

We walked most of that night and then slept in a little ravine and ate blackberries and our home made cakes during the day time which were rather soggy. The next night we moved on amongst endless thickets where paths made by woodcutters led into the deepest undergrowth and ended. We seldom found a path that led us for long in the right direction; we found plenty of water and some maize to eat. The Italian mountains are difficult to walk over in the dark, precipices, ravines, boulders and dense undergrowth all hamper movement and we had no compasses and no map except our own copies.

The next day at dawn we were walking through a beech forest and as the rising sun touched each trunk with a pentecostal flame it was quite beautiful and I felt free and happy for the first time. However, Italian peasants get up so early that we soon had to lie up amongst the roots of the trees, the woods were clear of undergrowth, hearing the woodcutters work all round us.

It started to rain in the afternoon. After dark we started off again, this time over very broken limestone country in continual danger of breaking our necks. The next day we lay up in a small thicket and brewed up, on a small margarine stove I had made, a cup of soup each. That evening, foolishly, we started off half an hour early, when it was still twilight, through some stone-walled tracks. We had not gone very far when we passed an Italian peasant. I said 'Good evening' and in reply to his question as to where we were going said 'Brienza' a town some miles away. Shortly after we were surrounded by half a dozen peasants armed with shotguns and axes, fortunately they kept the former pointed mostly at Jack, as with their fingers on the triggers and the butts in their shoulders they looked most dangerous. I replied to their taunts that we were two of the escaped British officers from Padula, by saying that I was not British and had never heard of Padula. I said with some conviction and I hoped with the arrogance that would be shown by one of the master race in the circumstances, that we were two German ship engineers from Salerno on a walking tour in the mountains. They refused to credit this statement and said that they had already been reprimanded by the Carabinieri that morning for letting someone who said he was a German through. They then said they would take us to the Carabinieri post. To this I replied there was nothing I would like more and that I would report them for their insolence when we arrived.

We had our identity cards copied from German ones and forged by a New Zealander in the camp in Indian ink. They were very well done with rubber stamp marks drawn in by hand and photographs cut out of German illustrated papers varnished over. It was difficult finding someone who resembled oneself. My photo was that of a German soldier with a brave but agonised expression on his face, his head tilted up being carried off the field at Stalingrad.

It was dark and realising that once we had reached the Carabinieri the game was up I crumpled my card and dropped it down my trouser leg as we were being marched along and Jack, did the same. If we were the first to be taken we did not wish to compromise the chances of the others.

On reaching the post it was empty. We were now surrounded by a crowd of villagers and one of their number was produced as an English speaker. I denied all knowledge of the language and said that I was fully prepared or able to go on speaking Italian. To this they insisted that I must know some English. I said that I knew some and after more pressure by the peasants and more evasion on my part I agreed to say what I knew. I turned to the man and very slowly and haltingly I said 'I love you Sweetheart.' The man looked somewhat surprised at this and turning to the crowd said: 'He doesn't know much English.' His presence however was a drawback, neither Jack nor I knew German and he did not speak Italian and we could now no longer talk in guttural English to each other, hoping it would pass as German.

To my horror they then said: 'Here is a man who speaks German.' I said 'Good evening' to him in Italian hoping to keep the conversation in that tongue. On pressure from the crowd he suddenly said: 'Habe brot.' I thought quickly, I could guess what that meant and felt I could better it, especially as we had had a concert in the camp a short time previously so I replied: 'Ja, ich habe Brot, gutten Abend, Bahnhof, Rosslein, Rosslein Rott.' He looked at the others and said: 'well he speaks German all right.'

Our prestige went up slightly and we were taken into a cottage and given bread and water after this. Then we were marched about three miles to another police post on a railway station, there was no one there either. Our guards, who being peasants probably had to get up excessively early in the morning now offered to let us go if we had any identity papers. It was too late and we had to admit that we had none. We were then marched along the railway for some ten miles, the Italians courteously carrying our haversacks and removing all the soap, razors and chocolate on the way, while they taunted us with the fact that one Italian soldier was worth ten English, and with the same cries that the Italian officers used that after the war the English who now ate five times a day would only eat once and the Italians who now eat one meal would then eat five daily. It was a tedious walk along the railway, the sleepers were always the wrong distance apart for walking, and we went through several tunnels.

We were taken to a Carabinieri post and then after a cross examination driven handcuffed together in the dicky of a car, by a rather charming Carabiniero, who kept his revolver in his hand, and told us he was very quick at the draw. We were deposited in the nearest town jail for the night and slept on a large inclined plank bed. The next day we were back inside Padula where we were cross-examined by a General who was certain we had contacts outside and wanted to know why we should wish to escape 'if we got to England we would only be sent straight to the front. How much better to stay in the sun drenched gardens of the monastery, sheltered from the evils of the War.'

Jack and I got thrown into the cell on our return where we found John Greenwood; during the course of the next few days Richard and Tom, Tony and Jack, Brian Smith all came in followed by the two New Zealanders.

The three youngest, Alan Hurst Brown, Roy Howard and Peter Bateman got as far as the Adriatic coast and were caught looking for a boat they could sail to Yugoslavia .

So we all did our seven days cells in Padula and were then transferred to Campo 5 [the Castello di Gavi, where he was to meet Peter Medd] where we stayed till after the Armistice. When, again on September 13th, John Redpath, Jack Craig and I succeeded separately in escaping, this time from the Germans, this time it was for good.

The tunnel had given us a full-time occupation and an incentive during the six weeks of its construction. It had made us unpopular with our fellow prisoners, particularly when we were all caught, and they accused us of only wanting to go and sit in the hills for a week as the result of which their wine ration had been stopped, that and the fact that we had not let everyone out the first night. But that was not our fault, we had agreed to seal the entrances to the tunnel so that the Italians wouldn't find them and we had done so.

However, Benincasa was Orderly Officer that night and on going round the upstairs dormitory he had discovered a dummy, the alarm was given. This was about three o'clock in the morning. All the prisoners were paraded in the Courtyard and on the instructions of the escape committee those who were answering for us and sleeping in our beds were told to answer their own names on Roll Call. The result of this was that the Italians soon discovered that out of thirteen prisoners missing, five were from Room 6. They searched the room very thoroughly, but they failed to find either the trapdoor or the hole in the field, so well had the two New Zealanders covered it with a board, sacking and earth.

As a result of our escape the Commandant was removed, Benincasa who was due for promotion remained a Captain, the tunnel diviner instead of his usual week's leave for discovering a tunnel got demoted and three sentries got a year's imprisonment each. Although our efforts to escape had failed we liked to think that as a patrol we had inflicted some casualties on the enemy.

*Lt. Col. F C Simms MC*
From *The* Antelope, *the Journal of the Royal Warwickshire Regiment*

# POEMS BY FRANK SIMMS

### Padula

House by house the village climbs
To stare across the walls,
To where we dream the days away
In cool and cloistered halls,
Or sunny walled-in garden
Beneath the olive trees
We sit amongst dark roses
And listen to the bees.

We do not hear the horror
Of this world's long travail;
The only sound we hear at night
Is singing nightingales
Whilst Scorpio seems striving
The crescent moon to touch
Bright stars which I in Africa
Had watched and loved so much
Up in the distant Mountain
Is quickly melting snow
And 'cross the everlasting hills
Great clouds and shadows go.

Near at hand we see the corn
With rapture bend and sigh
As the cool wind of sunset
Caressingly goes by.

We cannot reach that mountain,
Nor climb that village street,
The wire runs through the cornfield
And marks the sentries' beat.

Like flies encased in amber
Without delight or pain,
Futile and chill are all our days
Till we are free again.

### Requiem for soldiers and airmen fallen in the North African campaign

Blow softly winds of Africa!
The dead are close at hand:
Blow softly winds of Africa
Across the desert sand.

They have repaid the anguish,
The pains that gave them birth:
They have no need of sepulchre
Who died for all the Earth.
What want is there for flowers
While your great stars still shine?
They have no need for music
Whom silence doth confine.

From all the battling armies
Are gathered here the best.
Where none disturb their solitude
Where none disturb their rest.
They do not fear the screaming,
The shock, the searing blast,
For they have earned their freedom,
And now they sleep at last.

The splendour of the sunset,
The wonder of the dawn,
Will be for ever round them
When none are left to mourn.
The broken, bleeding bodies,
The twisted shattered bones,
Lie senseless now – unfeeling,
At rest beneath the stones.
Blow softly winds of Africa!
Above the brave set free.
Blow softly winds of Africa
Above the sounding sea.